Infusion of African American Content in the School Curriculum

Proceedings of the First National Conference

Editors

Asa G. Hilliard III

Lucretia Payton-Stewart

Larry Obadele Williams

Third World Press
P.O. Box 19730
Chicago, IL 60619

Second Edition
First Printing 1995

ISBN: 0-88378-153-0 Paper

Manufactured in the United States of America

Cover design by Angelo Williams

Third World Press
P.O. Box 19730
Chicago, IL 60619

ATLANTA PUBLIC SCHOOLS

The Southern Education Foundation, Inc.

Contents

Perspective

The 1989 National Conference on the Infusion of African and African American Content in the School Curriculum was designed to expose a very diverse general audience of educators and policy makers to a vital priority. *African people have played major roles in the development of world civilization, ancient and modern.* The Conference provided presentations that dealt with theory, issues, models, resources, structures, and networks that bear upon the effort to integrate this vital information into the regular school curriculum.

We learned that there is widespread interest in these topics and that many educators and interested citizens do not have ready access to the vast resources and experiences that are available now. We wanted to provide a saturation experience in the African and African American experience, so that all who came to the conference developed a grasp of what was available.

After years of systematic defamation, distortion and general neglect of the true experience and creativities of African and African American people, a vast amount of carefully researched and validated materials have become available. The work of many scholars, especially during the last 100 years, has provided us with the basis for a more accurate and fair picture of the true creativities and experiences of African and African Americans as a people in world history.

Our aim was to help provide the missing content that is multidisciplinary, holistic, thematic, and contextual. We want to see the story of a *people* told, not merely the story of isolated heroes and events. We want teachers to be able to tell an integrated story of continental and diasporan African people as it has evolved over time. It is this comprehensive story of African people that has affected world history and which is to be woven into the general school curriculum.

There is no conflict between curriculum infusion and special courses in ethnic studies. There are many ways to share this rich information and all ways must be exercised. The goal of the Conference and this publication is to provide the information base so that every way is possible.

We cannot predict all of the ways that Conference attendees will use their experiences from the Conference. We are convinced that the contributions of a very carefully selected set of presenters provided an experience that stimulated many positive activities. We hope that this effort was sufficiently worthy, and that it became a model for how the experiences of other geo-cultural groups can be tapped for an even greater enrichment of the general school curriculum.

Acknowledgements

Special thanks are extended to Dr. Elridge W. McMillan, president, Southern Education Foundation, and Dr. Herman L. Reese, conference consultant, Southern Education Foundation, their staff and volunteers for making the First National Conference on The Infusion of African and African American Content in the School Curriculum and its proceedings possible. The work of Dr. John Michael Palms, president, Georgia State University, the College of Education and the Department of Educational Foundations at Georgia State University are to be commended. The Atlanta Public Schools must be given thanks for its support of the conference and its vision. We are grateful to Mr. Carl Shivers for the conference photos used in this document, and to Mr. Alan Davis, graphic artist, for the conference logo art. And finally, a debt of gratitude is owed to Ms. Faye Bellamy, for transcriptions of addresses given during the conference. We extend our thanks to all of these individuals. Their efforts have contributed to a vision and hope for cultural equity in education.

Atlanta, Georgia
October 1990

Introduction

During the last weekend of October, 1989, the First National Conference on the Infusion of African and African-American Content in the School Curriculum was held in Atlanta, Georgia. It was convened under the co-chairmanship of Dr. Asa G. Hilliard, III and Dr. Lucretia Payton-Stewart, both of Georgia State University. The Department of Educational Foundations and the Department of Curriculum and Instruction of the College of Education at Georgia State University joined with the Atlanta Public Schools and the Southern Education Foundation in co-sponsorship of this national conference. Nearly 600 registrants from all over the United States and Canada came to participate in three intensive days of exposure to the vast wealth of information about African people worldwide. Public school teachers, university professors, school board members, foundation executives, publishers, representatives from the mass media and representatives from other interested segments of the general population attended. The conference was designed to be a saturation experience in the history and culture of African people in a diversity of academic disciplines. The organizers felt that it was important to offer information and documentation that would provide the basis for the design of African content that could be infused into the regular school curriculum.

Many efforts of this type have been initiated in local school districts and state departments of education over the years. Sometimes those efforts have been on a limited scale and parochial, at other times they have utilized the best scholarship that was available nationally and even internationally. Most often, however, curriculum work is done in a single discipline such as history or social studies, or it may fail to take advantage of the state of the art scholarship in the full variety of academic disciplines.

It was the hope of the organizers that the Atlanta experience would be seen first and foremost as an information resource rather than a final model of infused curriculum. Before infusion can take place, there must be a strong and appropriate data base. The conference should be seen as an approach to the answer to curriculum infusion problems that can be extended until we are satisfied that the very best in scholarship is provided as the foundation for curriculum recommendations. The conference entertainment, the commercial exhibits and all related activities were structured to support the overall purposes of the conference.

It is a well known fact that African people began to suffer from a devastating period of enslavement and movement to other parts of the world in the late 1400's. This vicious slave trade, initiated by the Portuguese, ultimately almost destroyed the social, economic, and political infrastructure on the African continent. The largest number of enslaved Africans were taken to South America, the West Indies and to North America. After a period of Arab slavery on the east coast of Africa, European colonization began around 1884. With a meeting of European nations in Berlin, a scramble for the possession of Africa by Europeans was begun. Even after slavery was declared illegal in most parts of the world, segregation and apartheid were created to continue the domination of African people by Europeans. Apartheid continues in South Africa to this very day.

Racism is a belief and behavioral system of oppression that grew out of the need to rationalize slavery, colonization and segregation. A component of racism was its destruction, distortion, and suppression of information. As the noted historian Dr. John Henrik Clarke, has said, "Europeans did not only colonize Africa, they would also colonize information about Africa." Few Africans or African-Americans were privileged to participate in the scholarship that related to their experience or to the experience of African people in relationship to other people. Even when such great scholars as W. E. B. DuBois, Edward Wilmot Blyden and Carter G. Woodson began to produce their great works of scholarship, the main stream academic world tended to ignore it. This has meant that the picture drawn by popular authorities of the experiences of African people has been grossly misrepresented. The legacy of that distortion is present in school materials and mass media that purport to represent the true experience of African people. As a result, it is important that a more truthful picture of the whole human experience be rendered, so that the actual place of African people in that experience can be presented without apology.

While it was not the purpose of the conference to deal directly with racism and its mechanisms and products, it is necessary to note that there is abundant scholarly literature on racism in the academic world. It is necessary to point to this body of literature in view of the fact that many Americans are not informed about the part that scholarship has played in the defamation of African people. Many lay people and many scholars have tended to believe that scholarship was neutral and objective. Perhaps no people have suffered more at the hands of such "neutral and objective" scholars as have people of African descent. A few illustrations will suffice to make the point.

> Speaking at the annual meeting of the Organization of American Historians, Leon Litwack, Professor of History at the University of California, Berkeley, and outgoing president of the organization, indicted past historians for perpetuating racism. He called on his present-day colleagues to heal that wound. . . .
> No group of scholars was more deeply implicated in the miseducation of American youth and did more to shape the thinking of generations of Americans about race and blacks than historians . . . whether by neglect or distortion, the scholarly monographs and texts they authored perpetuated racial stereotypes and myths. (Black Issues in Higher Education, 1987)

Professor Litwack was correct. Time and space will not

permit a full recounting of the level of involvement of some scholars in the misrepresentation of the experience of African people, however, a few illustrations will suffice.

Unknown to most people is the major part that Africa played in the development of human civilization. At one point in Western History, this role was well-known and recorded. However, for reasons to be explained, the following represents scholarly expressions of opinion about Africa, especially the history of Ancient Kemet (Egypt). Ancient Kemet was a native Black African nation. The culture associated with that nation existed for over 3,000 years as an intact civilization, beginning before the founding of Kemet and lasting well past native African independent control over it. In the late 1700's, scholars began to deny that Ancient Kemet was African or that African people had been a part of the main population of Ancient Kemet.

> 1776 *David Hume* "I am apt to suspect the Negroes and in general all the other species of men (for there are four or five different kinds) to be naturally inferior to the whites. There was never a civilized nation of any other complexion than white, nor even an individual eminent either in action or speculation. No ingenious manufacturers among them, no arts, no sciences."
>
> 1812 *George Curvier* "... widely hailed in France as the Aristotle of his age, and a founder of geology, paleontology and modern comparative anatomy, referred to native Africans as the most degraded of the human races, whose form approaches that of the beast and whose intelligence is nowhere great enough to arrive at regular government." (p. 36, Stephen Jay Gould, The Mismeasure of Man)
>
> 1831 *F. Hegel:* "This is the land where men are children, a land lying beyond the daylight of self conscious history, and enveloped in the black color of night. At this point, let us forget Africa not to mention it again. Africa is no historical part of the ..." (He was never in Africa.)
>
> 1840 *Louis Agassiz*, Harvard, leading naturalist. "This compact continent of Africa exhibits a population which has been in constant intercourse with the white race, which has enjoyed the benefit of the example of the Egyptian Civilization, of the Phoenician Civilization, of the Roman Civilization ... and neverthe-

less that has never been a regulated society of black men developed on that continent . . ." (p. 47, Gould)

1844   Samuel George Morton, M.D.   Had two medical degrees, one from Edinburgh. When he died in 1851, the *New York Tribune* wrote that "probably no scientific man in America enjoyed a higher reputation among scholars throughout the world than Dr. Morton (Gould, p. 51). "Morton set out to establish (racial) rank on 'objective' grounds. He surveyed the drawings of Ancient Egypt and found that Blacks are invariably depicted as menials—a sure sign that they have always played their appropriate biological role." "Negroes were numerous in Egypt, but their social position in ancient times was the same then as it is now, that of servants and slaves." (He conducted famous skull studies.)

1860's   Samuel Baker: While looking for the source of the Nile, Baker wrote, "Human nature viewed in its crudest state as seen among savages is quite on the level with that of the brute, and not to be compared with the noble character of the dog. There is neither gratitude, pity, love or self denial, no idea of duty, no religion, nothing but covetousness, ingratitude, selfishness and cruelty."

1880's   Richard Burton: "The study of the Negro is the study of Man's rudimentary mind. He would appear rather a degeneracy from the civilized man than a savage rising to the first step, were it not for his total incapacity for improvement. He has not the ring of the true mental. There is no rich nature for education to cultivate. He seems to belong to one of those childish races never rising to man's estate, who fall like worn out limbs from the great chain of animated nature."

1904   G. Stanley Hall, Founder of the *American Journal of Psychology*, and first president of the American Psychological Association believed that "certain primitive races, like children, are in a state of immature development and must be treated gently and understandingly by more developed peoples." Thus in his widely read work, *Adolescence*, Hall described Africans, Indians, and Chinese as members of 'adolescent races' in a stage of incomplete growth." (Gould, p. 7)

In *1856 Putnam's Monthly* reported, "the most minute and the most careful researchers have as yet failed to discover a history or any knowledge of ancient times among the Negro races. They have invented no writing; not even the crude picture-writing of the lowest tribes; they have no gods and no heroes, no epic poems and no legends, not even simple traditions. There never existed among them an organized government; they never ruled a hierarchy or an established a church."

Many scholars have refuted these statements with data. It is worth noting that many of these highly respected scholars who expressed these opinions, had never done empirical studies of Africa. Perhaps the most recent examination of this issue was done by Dr. Martin G. Bernal.

Recently, Bernal, grandson of the great Egyptologist Sir Alan Gardiner, and Professor at Cornell University, wrote the book *Black Athena* (1987). Dr. Bernal's book was a recent addition to the long tradition of African revisionist history. In the fourth chapter, entitled "Hostilities to Egypt in the 18th Century," Bernal explains how the ancient view of a highly developed and respected African civilization was modified through scholarship for political reasons:

"We are not approaching the nub of this volume and the origins of the forces that eventually overthrew the Ancient Model, leading to the replacement of Egypt by Greece as the fount of European civilization. I concentrate on four of these forces: Christian reaction, the rise of the concept of 'progress,' the growth of racism, and Romantic Hellenism. All are related, to the extent that Europe can be identified with Christendom. 'Christian reaction' is concerned with the continuation of European hostility and intensification of the tension between Egyptian religion and Christianity. . . . In the long run we can see that Egypt was also harmed by the rise of racism and the need to disparage every African culture; during the 18th century, however, the ambiguity of Egypt's racial position allowed its supporters to claim that it was essentially and originally 'white.' Greece, by contrast, benefited from racism, immediately and in every way, and it was rapidly seen as the 'childhood' of the 'dynamic' European race." (Bernal, *Black Athena*, 1987, p. 189)

Dr. Bernal goes on to show that a single prestigious university, Goettingen, housed a faculty, a large segment of which led in an academic assault on documented ancient history. This same university was highly influential and was responsible for the development of the field of study later to be known as "The Classics." According to Bernal's study, this development had much to do with the development of academic support for German nationalism. British universities followed the lead of Goettingen.

Some years ago, I came across a fascinating book about the professorate in Germany under Hitler. Weinreich (1946) wrote:

> "This murder of a whole people was not perpetrated solely by a comparative small gang of the Elite Guard of the Gestapo, whom we have come to consider as criminals. As is shown by Hitler's threat, afterwards frequently repeated by himself and his henchmen, as the literature of the Nazi Party, the Reich government, and the Wehmacht shows, the whole ruling class of Germany was committed to the execution of this crime. But the actual murderers and those who sent them out and applauded them had accomplices. German scholarship provided the ideas and techniques which led to and justified this unparalleled slaughter . . .
>
> The ideas underlying the ultimate 'action' were developed in advance with the necessary philosophical and literary trimmings, with historical reasoning, with maps and charts, providing for the details with well-known German thoroughness. Many fields of learning, different ones at different times according to the shrewdly appraised needs of Nazi policies, were drawn into the world for more than a decade: physical anthropology and biology, all branches of the social sciences and the humanities—until the engineers moved in to build the gas chambers and cemeteries." (pp. 6–7, Hitler's Professors: The Part Scholarship in Germany's Crimes Against the Jewish People)

These quotations are a way of announcing at the outset that the issues that concern us here are life and death issues. They are as much matters of truth and falsehood as they are matters of omission, prejudice, and stereotypes. The opening of the American mind must be a high priority topic. Curriculum issues for the public schools and for the universities that prepare teachers for those schools strike at the very heart of what the nation is all about.

Universities and public schools are at the center of the social construction of reality. What people come to regard as real and as legitimate will be greatly influenced by scholars and teachers. The mind of the nation is bound to the mind of its universities and schools, and also to its media industry and religious institutions. Artists, poets, novelists and musicians are also a part of the grand conversation. It is not useful to discuss which sector has the most influence. Suffice it to say that the universities have awesome power. For "power," as Dr. Wade Nobles has so often said, "is the ability to define reality and to get others to respond to that definition as if it were their own."

As shown above and in many other publications, universities are not neutral places. They are influenced by the same forces, economic and political, that impinge upon society at large. They often serve vested interests, even though the ideal is one of objectivity and neutrality. Where we find people in the depths of oppression, such as in South Africa today, free thought in the university will be a casualty. The more free the political order, the more free and open the academic mind.

Not all scholars reported on the experience of ancient Africans in this negative and false way. Some European and African, and African-American scholars wrote as follows.

1787 *Count C. F. Volney* (U.S. 1797) "There a people, now forgotten, discovered, while others were still barbarians, the elements of the arts and sciences. A race of men now rejected from society for their *sable skin* and *frizzled hair*, founded on the study of the laws of nature, those civil and religious systems which still govern the universe.

1952 *Thomas Hodgkin*, Former Secretary to Oxford University Delegacy for Extra-Mural Studies and a Fellow of Balliol College, Oxford, writing in *The Highway* of February 1952 said, "It is no doubt flattering to our vanity to imagine that the peoples of Africa were 'primitive' and 'barbarous' before the penetration of the Europeans, and that it is we who have 'civilized' them. But it is a theory that lacks historical foundation. The empire of Ghana flourished in what is now French West Africa during the dark ages of Western Europe. By the fifteenth century there was a university at Timbuktu. . . . The thesis that Africa is what Western European missionaries, traders, technicians and administrators have made it is comforting (to Western Europeans) but invalid. The eruption of Western European Colonizers into Africa—with all the effects of their religion and their schools, their gin and their guns, their cotton goods and their systems of administration—is only an event, though a very important event, in the history of African peoples.

If, therefore, we wish to understand the national movements that have emerged in Africa—and have reached their most mature and advanced stage in West Africa—we have to begin by trying to rid our minds of the European preconceptions that influence our thinking on this subject. This is not easy, since most of the available material on African affairs is presented from a European standpoint—either by imperial historians (who are interested in the record of European penetration into Africa), or by colonial administrators (who are interested in the patterns of institutions imposed by European governments upon African societies), or by anthropologists (who are often, though not always, mainly interested in the forms of social organization surviving in the simplest African communities, considered in isolation from political developments in the world around them). We shall probably have to wait a little while for the real history to Africa to be written by African scholars for an African reading public," quoted from *African Glory*, de Graft-Johnson, 1954.

In 1972 *Dr. John H. Clarke* stated, "The Europeans were no strangers to Africa, and this was not their first meeting. But in order to justify the slave trade, they had to forget, or pretend to forget, all that they had previously known about Africa. They had to forget that a lot of the early culture of Europe has an African base. They also had to forget that there were periods when Africans and Europeans lived in comparative harmony and Europeans married into African royalty. The Europeans had to forget that the Africans had a history and a heritage that could command respect."

Much more could be said about racism and scholarship. However, that is not the purpose of this document. It merely underlines the urgency for attention to the tasks of reconstruction of truth in history. For example, the history of African people, and especially the history of African-Americans, as presently presented in the public schools and institutions of higher education is deficient in at least six fundamental ways.

1. *There is no significant history of Africans in most academic disciplines before the slave trade.* In the total school experience of most Americans, virtually no attention is paid to the major part of the history of African people, even though that history is integrally tied to the history of humanity. For example, the history of early man, the history of the role that Africa played in the rise of early civilization, the history of Africa's part in world leadership in ancient times, and the history of the powerful influence of Africa on European culture is completely ignored.

2. *There is virtually no "People" history.* The history of African people is presented, if at all, in episodes and fragments of post slavery. Nowhere during the course of school curricula can students gain a sense of holism about the descendants of Africans and place Africans in their evolution with continuity and thematic treatment. African people, generally, are decontextualized. Person history is sprinkled almost as an affirmative action quota in some textbooks. People history is virtually absent.

3. *There is virtually no history of Africans in the African Diaspora.* Students do not get a sense that the descendants of African people are scattered all over the globe. As a result, many are shocked to find African populations in Brazil, Fiji, in the interior of the Philippines, and in Dravidian India, as well as many other places on the globe. They have no sense of where Africans are nor when or how they arrived at these locations.

4. *There is no presentation of the cultural unity among Africans and the descendants of Africans in the Afri-*

can Diaspora. Treatments of African people almost universally tend to emphasize physical and cultural differences among Africans. While there are differences, just as Europeans differ, many are quite superficial. What is overlooked is the deep structural cultural unity that can be found among many African populations all over the world.

5. *There is generally little to no history of the resistance of African people to the domination of Africans through slavery, colonization, and segregation apartheid.* Students could easily get the idea that African people were passive in the face of oppression and would have few, if any, role models for resistance to oppression if they relied on material presented in their schools. African resistance to oppression throughout the world has been vigorous, continuing and unrelenting.

6. *The history of African people that is presented fails to explain the common origin and elements in systems of oppression that African people have experienced, especially during the last 400 years.*

The goal of African and African-American curriculum infusion is to provide information that will assure that students are presented with a more total truth about the human experience. African-American curriculum infusion does not seek to replace one academic chauvinism with another to create false pictures of African people merely for the purpose of ensuring balanced representation. African people are a normal and natural part of the human experience that should be reflected in all academic subjects. As a result, our conference's focus was *multidisciplinary.* Though all academic disciplines could not be represented, it was the goal of conferees to show, through selected representations, a model for inclusion of African content in all academic disciplines. Presentations such as that by Dr. Wade Nobles provided a theoretical overview for an approach to curriculum development. Two other presentations, one by Dr. Ramona Hodge Edelin and the other by Dr. Johnnetta Cole, dealt with functions of culture in the education process. These presentations helped to place history as culture in the context of support for group development. Powerful presentations on the general history of African people by Dr. John Henrik Clarke, the history of Africans in art by Dr. Robert Farris Thompson, the history of Africans in the Western Diaspora by Dr. Richard Long, and the history of Africans in science and invention by Dr. Ivan Van Sertima gave both breadth and depth to the plenary sessions. The plenaries were augmented by presenters who extended certain plenary topics and who also offered models of implementation that could be considered by conferees.

One might extract seven generic objectives for a curriculum infusion process. Each of these objectives was supported by some aspect of the conference.

1. *A Story.* The story of African people must first be conceived in holistic terms. Answers to the questions posed by Booker T. Washington Coleman, a Washington D.C. educator and historian, should be provided. He asked that African children be able to ask the questions "Who in the world am I; where in the world am I; and how in the world did I get here?" These questions must be answered for African people generally. It is only after such questions have been answered that a content foundation can be provided for proceeding to additional objectives.

2. *Master the Stories.* All teachers in every academic discipline should have a basic mastery of this entire African story. In other words, teachers need a repertoire of content and principles of the African story which will allow them to use such curriculum materials as may be developed. Teachers, after all, are professionals, and one of the chief characteristics of a professional is the exercise of judgment. Curriculum materials cannot nor should they be made teacher

proof. However, if teachers are to use their judgments in the use of materials, the judgment can only be appropriate if it is rooted in a fundamental understanding of the general content of the story of African people.

3. *Use of the Stories in Curriculum.* Given the articulation of a story and the preparation of faculty in the understanding of that story, then curricula can be developed in scope and sequence for each academic discipline in order that an interdisciplinary understanding of this story be transmitted to students.

4. *Support Base.* Once curriculum infusion strategies have been developed, a support base for this effort must also be provided in schools that offer such curricula. Appropriate books, videotapes, maps, artifacts, film, audio materials, charts and graphs must be provided. In addition, conferences, resource peoples, field trips and special programs must be provided. Resource people must be identified. Any serious effort to rectify 400 years of academic wrong must be supported by appropriate sources of information and by a major effort.

5. *Creating Resources.* Professionals, community supporters and students should be enlisted to extend the development of curriculum materials by producing portfolios, film materials, videos, etc. as a creative contribution to curriculum development.

6. *Community Awareness and Participation.* In order for a community to support the curriculum infusion effort, it is absolutely essential that a community information process be developed and that the participation of the community in the work that the school does be invited and supported.

7. *Build a Structure for Continuity.* Anyone who is familiar with educational systems realizes that structural change is the only change that has an after life. Too often, innovations appear and in a flash are gone.

Organizational development principles must be utilized in building structures for continuity. This, of course, calls for deep structural training for professional staff and also for technical assistance of staff as they attempt to implement curriculum.

In a variety of ways, the Atlanta conference planners attempted to provide opportunities for discussion and presentation of models of how to approach strategies for curriculum infusion.

Keynote presentations from the conference provide the content for this volume. Many of the workshops offered excellent materials that could enhance the worth of this volume. However, we have chosen to go forth with the original plan to publish the plenary papers along with reference and research material. It is our hope that this beginning will provide a stimulus to those who understand the clear and pressing necessity to provide something of value to all our children. The African and African American infusion process is only a part of an even larger task that lies before us. Other geo-cultural groups have been slighted in the curriculum process. Similar efforts must be mounted in order for us to have a comprehensive picture of the true human story.

SECTION I
THEORY AND RATIONALE

Colonialism imposed its control of the social production of wealth through military conquest and subsequent political dictatorship. But its most important area of domination was the mental universe of the colonized, the control, through culture, of how people perceived themselves and their relationship to the world. Economic and political control can never be complete or effective without mental control. To control a people's culture is to control their tools of self-definition in relationship to others.

—Ngugi Wa Thiong'o

Wade W. Nobles, Ph.D.
Professor of Black Studies
San Francisco State University

Dr. Nobles is an experimental social psychologist with a special interest in the social, ethnic and cultural relativity of social science, research and evaluation models. He is a prominent theoretical scientist in the fields of African Psychology, cross-cultural and ethnic functioning. His research interests include African-American family dynamics, the psychological aspects of mythology, black child development, parenting and systems of human transformation and development. Dr. Nobles is the author of several works, including *Understanding the Black Family: A Guide for Scholarship and Research*. He earned his doctorate at Stanford University.

The Infusion of African and African-American Content: A Question of Content and Intent
by WADE W. NOBLES

THE ROLE OF CULTURE IN EDUCATION

Most mainstream American educators and scholars have rendered the relevance of culture to education as, at worst, the "something" which is really irrelevant to the task of education and should be disregarded (i.e., I don't see color, we should just teach children, etc.). At the other end of the cultural chauvinism continuum is the position that some cultures, at best, are deviant and should be replaced, or are deficient and should be strengthened before they can serve or address the educational agenda or curriculum concerns. In this latter case, the culture of a particular group becomes akin to a specialized subject matter and thereby a feature or component of the curricula. In this regard, the importance of culture is reflected in the curriculum by it (the curriculum) being sensitive to the ethnic heroes and holidays and aware of the groups songs and dance. Culture is not, however, simply a compilation of ethnic heroes and holidays nor is it only an awareness of other people's music and dance.

Following these trends, the exact influence of culture on curriculum has for the most part been elusive and evasive. Curriculum specialists and developers alike have attempted to address the issue of culture by either adding items of "cultural interest" to the curriculum or by attempting to develop cultural-free lesson plans. In either case the importance of culture is not adequately served. Curricula are tools of education and part of the problem has been in the way culture in general and African and African-American culture in particular, has been defined and applied to the educational experience. The driving force for most of our educational history, relative to culture, has been the erroneous belief in the homogeneity of American culture and the disdain and inability to recognize and respect African and African- American culture. Hence, cultural domination in the guise of acculturation and assimilation has been the *modus operandi* for American education and curriculum development.

Technically, culture is the vast structure of behaviors, ideas, attitudes, values, habits, beliefs, customs, language, rituals, ceremonies and practices peculiar to a particular group of people which provides them with a general design for living and patterns for interpreting reality. The system of culture teaches the people to recognize phenomena and to respect certain logical relations amongst phenomena. Culture gives meaning to reality. As such, culture has the power to compel behavior and the capacity to reinforce ideas and beliefs about human functioning, including issues of educational achievement and motivation. As such, culture is the invisible medium in which all human functioning occurs. It is important to note, in fact, that nothing human happens outside of culture. To think of culture as the medium in the Petrie dish is an appropriate analogy. It is the stuff in which human development occurs. Culture is to humans as water is to the fish. It is our total environment. As such, education as well as curriculum development are cultural phenomena. Culture is therefore the invisible dimension of all curricula. Hence, just as the nature of the water (i.e., salt vs. fresh vs. polluted) influences the reality (i.e., survivability) of particular types of fish, so too do different cultural systems influence the reality of particular groups of people.

In fact, all of our training and education are bound by what we call customs or professional conventions, which are nothing more than cultural traits or rituals. Culture is like our water, and like "the fish out of water," some humans can be out of their culture and thereby act inappropriately or fail to thrive. In a similar analogy, culture is like the electricity that illuminates the light bulb. We can only "know" or "understand" the electricity by what it does. Accordingly, if we are going to have a practice of education that's appropriate for African-American children, then it should be clear that we need to understand the "electricity" that's going to guide that practice.

An Explanation of the Technical Specifications of Culture

In regard to education, culture is not simply a compilation of ethnic heroes and holidays. Culture is also not simply an awareness of other people's music and dance. Oftentimes educators, unfortunately, see culture as the ingredient which "enriches" their standard educational presentation. Accordingly, if we are going to have African and African-American culture, let us figure out how we can throw in a few "Malcolm X's," a few "Sojourner Truths" or a few "Chaka Zulu's." We think as if culture in education means that all we have to do is make people "culturally sensitive" to the fact that Black folks like to dance or that Black folks like music or that brothers do have those big beep boxes or that music and dance is an essential part of the cultural aesthetic of Black folks. Infusing the content should not mean that we, as educators, should be satisfied with simply throwing into the curriculum African and African-American heroes and holidays as if we were seasoning soul food rather than managing the educational experience of culturally distinct children. When we do this we fool ourselves into believing that we have addressed the question of culture in terms of educational practice or experience.

Educators and scholars have used culture as a "feature" or "component" or an "aspect" of the human experience just like history or geometry. If they can't make culture an add-on feature of the "classroom drama," then they embrace a framework or set of assumptions that argue that putting African-American culture into the educational equation is optional or even counter-productive. In this latter regard, it is believed that African-American culture needs to be replaced. Educators, accordingly, spend a lot of energy trying to figure out how to replace or nullify the influences of African-American culture. In the behavioral sciences literature, this is referred to as the assumption of "cultural deviancy." Guided by the cultural deviancy belief, many educators assume that there is something "bad" about Black folks' culture and therefore attempt to change or replace it.

As another erroneous expression of the same notion, many educators have also implicitly argued that the culture of Black people is weak or lacking something in terms of the educational enterprise. Therefore, it (the culture) needs to be strengthened. The strengthening of culture in education is reflected by the strategy of sprinkling in heroes, role models and dance. The argument here is that there is actually a "cultural deficit," and all we as educators have to do is to reduce the deficit. There is also a third approach in education that says culture is essentially "whimsical." In this regard, it is believed that African-American culture is really irrelevant to the educational process. Educators simply disregard culture because it has no place in the business of educating children. Culture does not enter into the equation. Hence, we become *acultural* in the realm of education.

Parenthetically, we could point out that we as African-American educators, practitioners and administrators, have a unique and peculiar relationship with culture. It is almost a dilemma. In many respects our own professional success was contingent upon us putting the cultural integrities that we know in a box marked "Personal and Private." Once we become successful (i.e., make it through the system) it becomes very difficult to bring it out and talk about using it to educate Black children. That is our personal dilemma and I hope that we struggle with that at some point, because we can never approach and appreciate the real value of African-American culture when our own professional success has required that we deny the value of our culture. If we do not solve the dilemma, then what we do later on is always going to be tainted.

Unfortunately, when culture, in general, enters the educational debate it often becomes cast with the issue of access. The question then becomes, can we use cultural differences of people to inspire or to create a better method for accessing children into the core curriculum? For instance, do we see cultural differences as inhibiting access or do we see cultural awareness as increasing access? The fact of the matter is that when we look at the notion of culture and raise the question of accessing children to a core curriculum, we should be very clear that the *core curriculum* itself is cultural; and that the *teaching methodology* that we utilize in teaching the core curriculum is also cultural; and that the *site leadership style* is cultural, and that the *guidance and counsel techniques* are cultural, and that the *instructional strategies* are cultural, and that the *school climate* is cultural, and that ultimately the *aim and purpose of education* itself is cultural.

In fact, if we understand the issue of culture, we should see that it is not a "social product" (i.e., something we can add on to what we are doing) and that culture is really the total human process. As the everything of human reality, culture in education becomes how we use the "spirit and the energy" of a people.

I. INFUSING CULTURE IN CURRICULA CONTENT:

Culture, although, invisible, does influence the development of curricula, and cultures are reflected in the content of all curricula. Hence, regardless of the purpose of the curricula, the culture of the target group, must be taken into account if the curricula is to have full utility for that cultural group. This is true because curricula is in fact a human, and therefore cultural, activity. Technically speaking, curricula is a course of study whose purpose is to (1) systematically guide the transmission of information and knowledge, (2) reinforce the desire to learn/know and (3) encourage the internalization of behavior and/or attitudes consistent with the knowledge learned. The latter two tasks of curricula are almost always omitted in the discussion of curricula development. A curricula infused with African and African-American content[1] must systematically guide the transmission of information and knowledge while simultaneously reinforcing in African-American students the desire to learn and encouraging the adoption of behaviors and attitudes consistent with the historical excellence of African people.

A. When our curriculum deals with mathematics,
   it is important to infuse the curricula knowledge highlighting:

   1. The role of mathematics in classical African civilizations
   2. The importance of numbers in African theology and music
   3. African mathematical games
   4. The central role of the African (Muslim) mathematician Abu Kamil in the development of modern mathematics

B. When our curriculum deals with Language Arts
   it is important to infuse the curricula with information documenting:

   1. *The context of Black art:* To note that works of African art are personal expressions of collective reality and never art for art's sake.
   2. *The historical development of Black art:* There is a de-

---

[1] However, since culture is essentially a process which gives a people a general design for living and patterns for interpreting reality, if the curricula is not consistent with the people's general design for living and patterns for interpreting reality, then the curricula will also be inconsistent in its ability to guide the transmission of the intended information to reinforce the desire to learn and encourage internalization.

monstrable unbroken continuity in African art from Ancient Kemet to modern Black America.

3. *The functional continuity in African art:* The importance of symbolism, meaning and innate knowledge and the connection between the invisible and the visible as depicted in our art forms.

C. When our curriculum deals with *science*
it is important to infuse the curricula with information highlighting:
- Science and technology in the Nile Valley
- Understanding what the Ancients meant by 'Sacred Science'
- The African development of the first scientific paradigms
- The African use of time and the calendar
- The Dogon astronomical sciences
- African psychoenergetics
- The African roots of metallurgy and electrical engineering

Why is it important to do this? Because it situates us irrevocably on the stage of Humanity. In fact, by doing so, we consciously reaffirm our meaning as humans. Culture is the core and fundamental quality of human beingness and becoming. *By infusing African and African American content in the curricula, we, in effect, reaffirm the inalienable right of African people to (1) exist as a people; (2) contribute to the forward flowing process of human civilization (as contributors and not debtors) and (3) share with as well as shape the world (reality) in response to our own energy and spirit.*

Infusing African and African-American content in the curricula is, however, only half the charge. We must also see the need to infuse African and African-American culture into curricula intent.

II. INFUSING CULTURE INTO CURRICULA
INTENT:
The Question of Content and Character

By definition, character is the mark of someone or something which signifies its distinctive quality. Character is the complex of mental and ethical traits marking a group or nation. It is the detectable expression or evidence of the processes which control the transmission of one's hereditary information and nature. Hence, the curricula question must also address the issue of how we infuse the curricula content so as not to violate the mark of a people. How can curricula content assist in the development of the something which signifies the distinctive quality of a people? If our interest is in infusing African and African-American content in the curricula, then how can we infuse in the content of the curricula that which will stimulate and/or reinforce the growth and development of African and African- American mental and ethical traits, ergo character?

There is a RELATIONSHIP between CULTURE and BLACK STUDENT ACHIEVEMENT.

A Classical African Model

Classical African civilization and culture existed in a time when African people stood up and taught the world that they were conscious and Divine.

Education and curricula content as well as curricula intent was governed by the principles consistent with the Cardinal Virtues of Ma'at:

> **Truth**
> **Justice**
> **Righteousness**
> **Harmony**
> **Balance**

Propriety
Order

Under African educational curricula intent, excellence was achieved through education by focusing on:

A. A particular attitude and method for education

Primary	Secondary
CHARACTER	READING
COMMITMENT	WRITING
CONSCIOUSNESS	ARITHMETIC

B. The Afrocentric goal of education
   GOAL OF EDUCATION (harmony, understanding and enlightenment) is to assist in the development of a child who is:

   1. *COMPETENT*: demonstrates a level of skill indicative that s/he has the ability to do something well (human conduct)
   2. *CONFIDENT*: Exhibits an attitude and approach to life which reflects the belief that s/he is capable of doing anything (social responsibility)
   3. *CONSCIOUS*: Has an awareness of who s/he is, their purpose and path to fulfillment (moral character)

C. The process of education
   The educational process was not seen only as acquiring knowledge;
   it was seen as a *PROCESS OF TRANSFORMATION* of the learner or initiate, who progressed through successive stages of **re-birth to become** *EXCELLENT* (Godlike).
   At the place called Ipet-Isut (the most select of places),
   Black educational activity housed an elite faculty (called *herse-*

tha = teachers of the mysteries) or priest-professors. There were 80,000 students at all grade levels studying:

1. **The Heavens** (astronomy and astrology)
2. **The Lands** (geography)
3. **The Depths** (geology)
4. **The Secret World** (philosophy and theology)
5. **The Pharaoh** (law and communications)

Student achievement emphasized and was reflected in the students' human conduct, social responsibility and moral character.

D. African method of teaching character
   The ancient method of teaching character in order to develop competence, confidence and consciousness

   1. **Esoteric Instruction** (*Overt & Intentional*)
      Training man's sense and mind by applying the "Laws of Ma'at" (truth, justice, righteousness), the goal of which is to bring about understanding of:
      a. the conformity of the name of each thing with its true nature.
      b. the conformity of the appearance given to manufactured things (i.e., shape, color, decoration, etc.) with their purpose and function.
      c. the conformity of a building's measurement and proportions with the laws it was meant to teach.

   2. **Esoteric Instruction** (*Symbolic and Subliminal*)
      Training man's senses and mind to interpret the signs and symbols in reality by understanding:
      a. the lessons of Thoth & Seshat
      b. the neter of writing, geometrical patterns and shapes occurring in nature
      c. the configuration and signature in which everything on earth reveals its characteristics and properties

III. TRAINING METHODOLOGY

A. *ACCENTUATION* of a characteristic in some species/individual.

B. *ASSOCIATION* within one scene of certain plants and animals which live in symbiosis.

C. *ATTRIBUTION* giving to each being a name composed in such a way that everything that lives on the earth, in two heavens and in the Dwat[2] should have its nature implied (revealed) by its name.

IV. THE TEACHING OF THE SCIENCES

A. The science of man

1. His physical body
2. The psychic being
3. The meaning of human life
4. Destiny beyond the grave

B. The science of nature

1. The elements & their symbolism
2. The science and nature
3. Knowledge of seasons and of nature

C. The science of the universe

1. Astronomical teaching
2. Cosmogony (theogony—theology) three aspects:
   i. primordial creation
   ii. realization as manifestation (genesis)
   iii. achievement of creation
3. Training and secondary causes

---

[2] Dwat—The Kamites of Kemet called Dwat (from dwa, the moment between night and day); it is the world of transition between the abstract world of the casual powers and the concrete world of phenomena or world of nature. It is the state of everything which moves towards a 'becoming' or towards a 'return'.

D. The science of numbers, measurement and proportions

   1. The numerical/mathematical factor, "universal harmony"
   2. Perceptive spirit
   3. Representative of the development or becoming of man

THE RESULTS OF THE INFUSION

When African people look honestly at our history regarding culture, what we in fact see is that culture has always been the hidden key to our educational excellence and our accomplishments in civilization. We can simply refer back to literally the beginning of time and look at the contributions of African people. History teaches us that from the beginning of time (approximately 6,000 years ago), during the first six dynasties of ancient Egypt, what is called the pyramid age, that culture was the hidden ingredient that allowed African people, our ancestors, to build permanent material structures and spiritual (social) systems that today everybody looks to in marvel and disbelief. Many don't even want to admit that Black men and women created the pyramids by utilizing our culture to stimulate educational excellence.

    I can also talk about the accomplishments of the 18th, 20th and 25th dynasties or look at the kingdoms of Ghana, Mali, or Songhai and recognize that the greatness of these moments were linked to cultural realities. The Moorish conquest of the Iberian Peninsula which ultimately led to Christopher Columbus getting an "endowment" to find the trade routes to the East was also driven by our culture. The standard core history curriculum has mislead us about the true facts. The Moorish conquest was a Black cultural experience that was tied to educational excellence.

    These were times when our cultural truths were orchestrated in the service of excellence. Culture was (is) the key to our contribution to world civilization. Tuskegee, Hampton, Howard, Morehouse, Spelman, Talladega, Morris Brown,

Florida A and M, Clark Atlanta University, etc., with all their inabilities and all their dependencies on various kinds of structures, continue to educate our children to excellence utilizing our culture. We need to look at this not to say that "Oh, Black folks did something good" but to learn from what are the hidden ingredients. It is not enough to simply infuse the curriculum with great African Kings and Queens.

This chart documents a sampling of African achievements overlooked in most curricula.

THE CONTINUUM OF AFRICAN CULTURE AND ACHIEVEMENT

DYNASTY I—VII	**Building of the pyramids**
6,000 BC	Established first university
Dynasty XVII	**Temples and tombs**
1587 BC	Centers of intellectual life
Dynasty XXV	**Restoration of "ancient**
700 BC	**ways"**
	Return to paths of Enlightenment
Ancient Kingdom of Ghana	**Trade and learning center**
700–1200 AD	Education key to commerce
Moorish Conquest of Iberian Peninsula	**Brought Europe out of "Dark Ages"**
1000 AD	Est: Cordova & Grenada
Ancient Kingdom of Mali	**Timbuktu the center of higher learning**
1200–1500 AD	
Ancient Kingdom of Songai	Learning/commerce center of life
1300–1600 AD	
Founding of Tuskegee Institute	**Est. African-American center of education**
1800's	Source of Black Achievement for Decades

V. THE APPLICATION OF CULTURE IN SERVICE OF CONTENT AND CHARACTER: THE CALIFORNIA EXPERIENCE

Clearly, there is something called *"culturally consistent educational praxis"* and African-American educators and practitioners must struggle with, clarify, sharpen and understand culturally consistent educational practice as we approach this question of turning around the educational failure of our children. Culturally consistent educational practice is a systematic process of developing and stimulating the knowledge, skill, ability, attitude and character necessary for students to undertake socially-defined, goal-oriented and culturally-meaningful activities. The process must be designed to develop a competent, confident and conscious human being whose educational achievement is reflected in h/er conduct (a content issue); social responsibility (a content and intent issue); and, morality (a character issue).

I believe that the merging of curricula content and curricula intent can be accomplished via what I think should be called "culturally consistent educational practice."

"Culturally consistent educational practice" is designed to allow our children to:

(1) achieve mastery of all aspects of human functions,
(2) to reproduce themselves in the objective world; and,
(3) to make explicit their character/personality.

What is the real character/personality of African people? What does it mean to be an African woman, an African man? What is the character type called Hapshepsut? What is the character type called Imhotep?

We need to know these principles so that we can begin to talk about learning from them. We need to know them, so that we can use the systems which created African genius and excellence as our prototype and marker or criterion for educational practice. It seems to me that there is a way to look at educational praxis that is different from simply adding on some holidays and sprinkling in a moment when Black children maybe can dance in the gym in the name of cultural enrichment.

The methodological steps in the infusion of African & African-American content and intent in school curriculum are as follows:

A. Provide an educational experience which unashamedly and unapologetically affirms and advances the*"human imperatives," "cultural pre-requisites"* and *"relational essence"* of the student's culture.

B. Provide an educational experience which is designed to encourage the student's constant participation in and immediate impact upon the development and positive transformation of cultural reality.

C. Provide an educational experience whose vision and purpose goes beyond the goal of acculturation and accommodation and instills in children the personal and collective desire to understand and influence the direction of world governance toward global cultural understanding and respect.

D. Provide educators with the skills and attitudes (i.e. feelings and beliefs) that culturally diverse children can learn and are worth every effort, every sacrifice and deserve every chance to develop their minds and human potential.

E. Help parents and teachers to understand each other's cultural truths and to share in the conviction that the children's cultural group is first and foremost responsible for the education, development and protection of the children.

F. Understand that education must be in the service of the people's right to determine their own history and the child's right to experience an educational environment which maximizes h/er human possibilities.

The right educational philosophy has to be tied to not only the six things mentioned above, it must also be tied to the recognition that in a modern, multi-cultural society, educators should be clear that we need to have a core curriculum that everybody should know, while allowing for different cultural integrities in the achievement of education. In effect, we need to work toward a monoliterate society by utilizing multi-cultural processes and methods. So as we approach Asian, African, European, and Indio (Mexican) children we use their cultural realities (i.e., images, energy and spirit) to determine as well as to guarantee that they receive the core body of knowledge that is necessary.

THE ROLE OF BLACK SCHOLARSHIP AND EDUCATION

A further and final rationale for infusion of content and intent is found in two ideas. The first idea is imbedded in the role of African scholarship and education. The role of Black scholarship is to create and constantly revise the formalized framework which guides the assessment and evaluation of reality in relation to African people. Our role as educators is in part to develop the perceptual, cognitive and affective achievements which represent our own authentic organizational plan for understanding and influencing the development of the African character.

Infusion of African and African-American content and intent in the curriculum by definition must be Afrocentric.

In terms of curricula content, the educational process should (1) refer to the life experiences, history and traditions of African people as the center of analyses; (2) utilize African and African-American experience as the core paradigm for human liberation and higher-level human functioning; and, (3) assist African-American students in the self-conscious act of creating history.

In terms of curricula intent, the educational process should (1) be grounded in the intellectual and philosophical foundation upon which we create the scientific criterion for authenticating African reality; (2) stimulate our ongoing quest for our own indigenous historical and cultural anchor; (3) reinforce a quality of thought and practice which is rooted in the cultural image and interest of African people. Finally, the content and intent of the curricula should simultaneously reaffirm the right of African people to (1) exist as a people; (2) contribute to the forward flowing process of human civilization and culture and (3) to share with as well as shape the world in response to our energy and spirit.

The second idea is captured by the following statement taken from *Everyday Classics* by Thorndike and Baker:

"We have chosen what is common, established, almost proverbial, what has become indisputably classic, what in brief every child in the land ought to know because it is good and other people know it. The educational worth of such materials calls for no defiance in an age when the need for socializing and unifying our people is keenly felt that the value of a common stock of knowledge, a common set of ideals is obvious. A people is best unified by being taught in childhood the best things in the intellectual and moral heritage. Our own heritage is like our ancestors, Hebrew, Greeks, Roma, English, French, Teutonic elements all blended in our cultural past. We draw freely from all of these. Introduction to the best of this is one of the ways of making good citizens."

Does the core curriculum or the educational practice implied by this profound statement include African-American people? If it does not, then it is not an application of our culture in the service of educational excellence. This quote is given in part by Hirsch as justification for his notion of "*cultural literacy.*" It in effect represents somebody's "bible" on what to do in educating children. Does this represent the best for African-American children? If your answer is no and you believe that this kind of thinking does not include African-American children, then consider the possibility that we can begin a process or an educational movement wherein educators can engage in a program of activity that systematically and passionately examines, develops and implements solutions to the education crisis of African- American children.

In California we have established the *Center for Applied Cultural Studies and Educational Achievement,* a University-based educational research, development and training center devoted to the identification, explication and application of culturally consistent educational pedagogy and praxis relative to African (Black) American educational excellence. The fundamental and primary mission of the *Center for Applied Cultural Studies and Educational Achievement* will be to systematically and continually:

(1) study the generic problems and issues which impact on the educational success of African-American students;

(2) determine the cultural and systemic requisites necessary for the effective education of African-American students;

(3) engage in an ongoing identification, evaluation and replication of applied culturally consistent educational techniques, methods, practice and programs relative to African-American educational excellence;

(4) develop authentic and/or innovative strategies, methods and techniques of effective, culturally consistent educational applications; and,

(5) design and implement a procedure and/or process for the institutionalization of proven, culturally consistent educational praxis at every level and aspect of the African-American educational experience.

We need a place where we can undertake the evaluation, validation, application and implementation of African-American culture in the education system.

Critical Terms & Definitions

Culture: Culture is a human process representing the vast structure of behaviors, ideas, attitudes, values, habits, beliefs, customs, language, rituals, ceremonies and practices peculiar to a particular group of people and which provides them with a general design for living and patterns for interpreting reality.

Core culture: The central portion/strand or essence of "the process which gives the group its general design for living and patterns for interpreting reality." It is the "essential spirit" or energy of the group which characterizes and is reflected in all processes consistent with the group's cultural reality, including educational content and methods.

Applied cultural studies: The utilization of cultural precepts, processes and laws to solve, guide and understand human functioning, requisites and imperatives relative to the stimulation, reinforcement and internalization of the educational process.

Culturally consistent educational praxis: A systematic process of developing and/or stimulating the knowledge, skill, ability, attitude and character necessary for the subject (student) to undertake socially defined, goal-oriented and culturally meaningful activity designed to allow them to achieve mastery of all aspects of human functioning, (re)produce themselves in the objective world, make explicit their personality, and validate their self and kind.

Multicultural education: "Multicultural education is an inter-disciplinary educational process rather than a single program. The process is designed to ensure the development of human dignity and respect for all peoples. An essential goal within this process is that differences be understood and accepted, not simply tolerated. Within this definition lie the

23

concepts embraced by cultural pluralism, ethnic and intercultural studies, and intergroup and human relations."

Educational (achievement) excellence: A level of accomplishment indicative of mastery of a skill, ability, character, knowledge or information representative of personal competence and sociocultural confidence.

Teaching style: A particular manner, method, way or form of (1) transmitting information and knowledge; (2) encouraging the learning process and (3) orchestrating a set of experiences designed to foster development and maturation.

Pedagogy: The art and science of teaching.

Curriculum: A course of study whose purpose is to (1) systematically guide the transmission of information and knowledge and (2) reinforce the desire to learn/know.

Core curriculum: A program of studies in which a number of courses are unified by and subordinated to a "central theme."

Growth and development: Any identifiable and measurable change which is locatable in time and space and recognizable by the senses.

Developmental experience: Any experience or set of experiences whose intention and/or consequence is to foster the growth and maturation of any aspect of human functioning, including teaching and learning.

Educational praxis: The means by which one self-consciously shapes the educational experience, its historical conditions and concrete outcomes relative to the specific interest and intent of a client community.

Educational excellence: A performance criterion relative to educational achievement wherein the goal is to "match the maximum" as distinct from "meeting the minimum" standards in student and/or school performance.

. . . the world outlook of a people is embodied in their moral, aesthetic and ethical values which are in turn embodied in their culture.

—Ngugi Wa Thiong'o

Johnnetta B. Cole, Ph.D.
President
Spelman College

Dr. Cole in 1987 became the first black woman to head Spelman College, Atlanta, GA. Prior to the Spelman appointment, she was a professor of anthropology at Hunter College and a member of the graduate faculty at the City University of New York. Dr. Cole did undergraduate work at Fisk University and Oberlin College, earning master's and doctoral degrees in Anthropology at Northwestern University. Her scholarship centers on Cultural Anthropology, Afro-American Studies and Women's Studies.

The Cultural Base in Education
BY JOHNNETTA B. COLE

My dearest sisters and brothers, I can't tell you what an honor it is to be a part of this expression of who we are. For you, for me, for all of us, let me begin by saying the warmest, the most sincere Asante! Asante! To those who have conceived and birthed and nurtured this idea, we can only give our gratitude and our commitment to leave here now and do the right thing.

May *Elegba* open the gates of our hearts and our minds. This is a great gathering. This is a great coming together in the interest of our tomorrows. That's our children. We need historic gatherings such as this. Books and papers have their place and their purpose, but there is a special power in imparting ideas face-to-face. Opportunities to speak directly with colleagues, with friends, with sisters and brothers can seriously inspire our thinking and remind us that Africans all over this planet are descendants of a long tradition of oral communications.

It is a tradition that pre-dates Western civilization and it is a tradition that perhaps more than at any time in history has a powerful role to play in an age of information. A gathering like this permits us to call out to each other, and importantly, we can respond. Indeed, call and response is the model of refined communications, a thing of beauty and of power. You know it when you hear it in our churches. When the call comes for an Amen and sometimes for an A *woman* too, you know it is call and response. Also when you hear it in classical Black music or, improvisational African American music. If there was ever a piece of poetry from the islands we call the Caribbean we know it goes back and forth like that water,

27

running in and out. When our brothers are on those fishing boats, when our sisters are lifting those hoes, the call comes and so does the response.

Call and response is the freedom of speech in its purest form. Every "amen," each, "teach now sister, take your time," every one of those "right on," even the negative shake of the head, and if no more than the list of that hand that goes back and forth register that the response is there. Each response shapes and colors the call. This is a process that empowers all of us. It is far less expensive than opinion polls.

In certain settings the dynamics of call and response is overlooked or misinterpreted. White American moviegoers have been known to complain that the bloods talk back to the moviescreen. We sure do. Even after centuries of an aborted attempt to assimilate all that is our culture, after centuries of misinformation, we Afro-Americans still respond to the right call. Respond we must. We cannot sit silent while others define our realities for us.

When those who are ignorant of our considerable contributions to civilization on this planet deny or denigrate us, we must respond in a strong, in a logical, in a self-determined manner. Education, if it is anything, is a response to ignorance.

We were correct, sisters and brothers, in the 1960s when we declared ourselves an African people. Today, 11 years before the next century, we need to declare it again. We are an African people.

We need to speak clearly of an African world. Not in an exclusive or a provincial sense, but as a factual reality. After all, humankind first walked on this earth, there, there on a continent now called Africa. It was there that our people lived with *Ogun*, with *Elegba*, with *Obatala*, with *Shango*, with *Oshun* and they came with us, those *orishas*. They came with us into this new world. Although in the Caribbean they may have been called St. Peter, St. Barbara, call 'em St. Whatever-youwill, they were *Obatala*, *Shango*, and *Ogun*.

Into this part of the African-American world, when that

twitch gets in that sister's neck, she raises that hand and says, "Ohhhh Jesus," the orishas have responded to the call. There are those who would argue that it is an African world in the world of Christianity where it is these orishas, where it is this set of profound beliefs out of our African cosmology that continue to breath the beauty and the tenacity into something called Christianity. If the truth be known, much of modern knowledge stands on the shoulders of ancient Africa.

Many scholars have been in the vanguard of the movement to restore credibility to our place. African American men and women have challenged the vicious assertion that somehow we stood on the shores of West Africa, dug our nails into our bodies and pulled out all that was African to come like sponges into the New World. No people on the face of the earth have ever done such an outrageous thing and neither did we.

Indeed, when the setting was Harvard and Brother Malcolm spoke on this notion of the cultural base of African American life, he expressed this sentiment. Malcolm said, "Now let me ask you somethin'. If you don't believe that Africa moves through us, let me ask you somethin', If a cat gives birth in an oven do you think it has biscuits?"

This conference has brought together our brother scholars and sister scholars who have refuted assimilationist claims that Africans in the Diaspora retain nothing of value that is African. You, our pioneering scholars, our beloved Asas and John Henriks, you have illustrated our retention of African culture despite consistent efforts to eradicate all traces of Africa from us. But we have been giving birth to kittens.

Yes we are an African people and this is an African world. We gather then at this conference, or we have almost finished gathering, this time, to design systems that will ensure that the world understands the significance of our declaration. We don't declare this an African world in order to collect royalties, and frankly, we don't have any time for idle boasting. We call for an enlightened world view because ignorance of the truth is the enemy of every human being who wants to live free.

Those of us who have been privileged enough to learn of African achievements and to know of African American accomplishments, we must teach. We must teach. And that teaching has to create a broader interest in a variety of outlets so that we reach far beyond Black History Month and a ritualized roll call of our heroes. We must create the method and the means of weaving African and African American content into the fabric of world discourse and action.

We do not seek the validation of Africa and the logical utilization of African wisdom at the expense of the Asian world. At the expense of the Latino world. At the expense of the European. At the expense of any world. In fact all worlds will benefit when the light of truth is focused on the so-called "Dark Continent," and when the country that is now ours too, finally comes to understand that we are perhaps one of its most important expressions of identity.

Let me turn now to say in a different way why we must indeed infuse African and African American cultural content into the school curriculum. Brother Reese did me a terrible deed. Not that he insisted that I come, but they put me at the luncheon after everybody had said everything. But that's alright. Whatever you've been saying throughout this conference let me now play the role that Brother Count Basie or Brother Duke Ellington would play and that is to lift it and say "One more time."

African American children and all of God's children, must be taught about Africa and about Afro-America so that they, one, may know themselves. Two, may truly know their country, and three, may bring to the world some of the most important lessons of our time. Our children must know themselves. "I am because we are. We are because I am." These African words capture the reality that our knowledge of ourselves as individual human beings is embedded in a sense of our peoplehood. To deny our African-American children a consciousness of themselves, through their people, is to cripple them psychologically and emotionally forever.

Why is it so hard to see that our children need to know

of the Kingdoms of Mali and Ghana and Songhay, know less than they know about Athens and Rome?

Why is it so hard to see that in their classrooms our children must meet themselves when they meet the good Dr. W. E. B. Dubois along with meeting other great thinkers and activists of American history. Our children must know the works of Margaret Walker and Chinua Achebe and George Lamming, no less than they know of Conrad or Hemingway or an Emily Dickinson?

Why is it so hard to see that our children need to know about traditional West African work groups, Caribbean cooperatives and African-American quilting bees?

Why is it so hard to see that our children need to know *Anasi* in Ghana? They need to find *Anasi* again in Jamaica, and watch out now, here comes *Anasi* called Brer Rabbit.

Why is it so hard to see that our children need to know that they are a great part of a long and continuous movement of ideas, of creativity, of passion, and of power?

"What shall we tell our children who are black?" Margaret Burroughs asks us to ask. "I tell you that we had better tell them that millions and millions of women and men who are black, stretching from women and men in the earliest of human forms in Africa through soldiers of freedom like Nanny of Jamaica, Toussaint l'Overture of Haiti and our own Harriet Tubman. Tell them those are their people."

Let us tell our children who are black, of Mae Jemison and Augusta Savage and Vernon Johns and yes, sisters and brothers of struggle of names we don't even know. If our children need to know and feel all of this for their own sense of being, of belonging, of worth, think how other children need to know it too so they will finally know who our children are.

Our children must truly know their country. "You will never know America until you come to grips with slavery." I heard somebody say that one day. The power of that statement has never left me. All of our children, black, brown, yellow, red, white, cannot know their country. They cannot know America without knowing the political economy and cultural history of Africa and of African-Americans. And they've got to know how Africa's children have been treated. They have got to know how we have been forced to be the least among us.

In New York City today, they tell me that 70 percent of the racist incidents that occur are being done by youths 19 years of age and younger. Who in the world is teaching them and in what schools? Our children, and we ourselves, cannot understand how this nation began and has prospered until it is clear who was stolen, who was raped, who was worked to death and who has been killed in the process.

To know all about Thomas Jefferson, but to know nothing of his mistress, our sister Sally, is not to know Jefferson.

To know the geopolitics of Europe, but not to know the Brazilians speak Portuguese, not Spanish, and that Brazil has the largest African American population in the world, is to be truly, Carter G., "miseducated." Teaching children about the immigrants who built America by references to Ireland, Poland and Greece, but never to Barbados, Jamaica, Trinidad and Haiti is to teach them far less than the whole story. Can America's children ever know America if they recite Robert Frost poems and can't give you some Langston Hughes?

Can America's children encounter what they need to know without understanding the centrality of Africa and Africa's people in the very formation of America. In America's most intense battles and indeed in America's ultimate destiny, stand we, my sisters and brothers. Our children must teach the world better.

When I think beyond the moment and place that we are in, when I set my thoughts on our world, I realize how desperately we need to right so many wrongs. I realize how we need to find peace but only if it comes with justice. I realize that we need to discover that diversity can and does beautifully coexist with equality.

But where will these lessons come from? I think that our world can learn an incredible set of lessons from confronting

African and African-American culture. We must teach our children so that our children can show the world that where there is oppression there is also resistance. Think of the barbarism of slavery, but then think about Nat Turner. Remember Jamaican Maroon societies and don't you ever forget that African-American sister singing "Steal Away."

Think of the horrors of apartheid in South Africa and then feel good when you think about the persistent anti-apartheid struggle of our African sisters and brothers and now the slow but sure sign that victory is a-coming.

We must teach our children so that our children can show the world, that in the words of the 19th Century Black Nationalist Martin Delaney, "To know the conditions of a people you have but to know the condition of their women."

The history or shall we call it herstory, of Black women in America is an extraordinary story of pain and triumphs of fads and style, of one, two or more jeopardies. It is the story of lifting while we climbed. It is a moving drama of Sojourner, of Mary Church Terrell, of Anna J. Cooper, of Mary McCloud Bethune, of Bessie Smith, of Zora Neale Hurston, of Lorraine Hansberry, of Barbara Jordan, of Toni Morrison and Marian Wright Edelman. There are all those sisters whose names we do not know, but the quality of their struggles makes them "sheroes" to us all.

How much, how very very much we African and African-American people can share with the world. Let me bring closure.

This conference is no small thing. How significant it is this coming together of Africa's people. Coming together with those who share our dream of infusing African and African-American content in the school curriculum. Welcome White sisters and brothers.

So I want to end with expressions of gratitude to all of the sisters and brothers who have brought us together and to those who responded when they called. If we do the work that we have imagined here, if we can bring about the changes that we have boldly called for, then we will be thanked by all of Africa's people, by all of the peoples of the world now and forevermore. And then one day, one day, when the call goes out to us "Are you free"? the response will come like the roar of the ocean, "Yes, thank God, we are at last." Asante.

It took an educational effort that was systematic, intensive, and unparalleled in the history of the world to erase these memories, to cloud vision, to impair hearing, and to impede the operation of the critical capacities among African Americans. Once reference points were lost, African Americans as a people became like a computer without a program, a spacecraft without a homing device, a dependent without a benefactor.

—Asa G. Hilliard III

Ramona H. Edelin, Ph.D.
President and Chief Executive Officer
The National Urban Coalition

Dr. Edelin has been associated with the Coalition since 1977, following an outstanding career as a social activist, scholar and academic administrator at leading institutions of higher education. She is often identified with the Coalition's "Say YES to a Youngster's Future" (TM)—an early intervention program that helps prepare minority youth for the high-technology jobs of the 21st Century. A Phi Beta Kappa Graduate of Fisk University, Dr. Edelin also studied at Harvard, earned her Master's in Philosophy at the University of East Anglia in Norwich, England, and her Ph.D. in Philosophy at Boston University.

Curriculum and Cultural Identity
BY RAMONA EDELIN

The key to unlocking the genius of our children, tapping into that talent bank which is so evident and glorious in arenas outside the classroom, is to be found in the relationship of curriculum to cultural identity.

An issue that was central to slavery, and to the establishment of an American apartheid which accompanied the defeat of the Reconstruction, was that of the identity of the African slave. Slaves were torn from their motherland; separated from their kin; denied and forbidden their names, customs and religion; and stringently prohibited from securing formal education or marriage. To the extent that it was possible, they were forced to face enslavement in a new land singly, one by one, alone and without even the understanding and promise which their families had infused into their highly personal names.

Though slavery as a concept was not new to the world, the African slave trade took applications of the military maxim, "divide and conquer" to its most elaborate extreme. The slave was identified by his enslavers not by his name, his home, his religion or family, but by his color—the one thing which he could not shed or change in order to assimilate, even if he wanted to.

Over the years, an African American identity has been formed which, though hardly monolithic and not free of the tensions and treasons which are endemic to the process of overcoming oppression and exploitation, can be clearly seen in the behaviors and preferences of the vast masses of our group. There is an identity; but it entails a built-in dilemma of intense proportions. DuBois puts it best:

It is a peculiar sensation, this double consciousness, this sense
of always looking at one's self through the eyes of others, of
measuring one's soul by the tape of the world that looks on in
amused contempt and pity. One never feels his two-ness, an
American, a Negro, two souls, two thoughts, two unreconciled
strivings: two warring ideals in one dark body, whose dogged
strength alone keeps it from being torn asunder. (W. E. B. Du
Bois, *Souls of Black Folk*. Chicago: A. C. McClurg, 1903; New
York: Fawcett, 1964, pp. 16–17)

This, then is the end of his striving: to be a co-worker in the
kingdom of culture, to escape both death and isolation, to hus-
band and use his best powers and his latent genius.

This waste of double aims, this seeking to satisfy two unreconciled ideals, has wrought sad havoc with the courage and faith
and deeds of ten thousand people—has sent them often wooing
false gods and invoking false means of salvation and at times
even seemed about to make them ashamed of themselves. (W.
E. B. Du Bois, *Souls of Black Folk*. Chicago: A. C. McClurg,
1903; New York: Fawcett, 1964, pp. 16–17) I began to feel that
dichotomy which all my life has characterized my thought: how
far can love for my oppressed race accord with love for the op-
pressing country; And when these loyalties diverge, where shall
my soul find refuge? (Du Bois, *Autobiography*, New York: International Publishers Company, Inc. 1968)

As the African American group looks today at its condition and its future, Du Bois' two-ness has a searing reality
and immediacy, resolving the dilemma of two-ness, evolving a
whole, self-sufficient and harmonious identity as a group, is
imperative at this time. Before cultural renewal can unfold,
before education can lead our group back to its ancestral mastery in learning, before the development of a self-sustaining
economic infrastructure can be effected, we must arrive at
an informed and inspired new understanding of who we are.
Making the most of being African in America can be a compelling creative challenge resulting in perfect equality if we
properly understand our possibilities and work toward fully
realizing them, together.

In Africa, family and tribal identification was definitive. In the New World, a remarkable adjustment was made:

> The final gift of African "tribalism" in the nineteenth century was its life as a lingering memory in the minds of American slaves. That memory enabled them to go back to the sense of community in the traditional African setting and to include all Africans in their common experience of oppression in North America. It is greatly ironic, therefore, that African ethnicity, an obstacle to African nationalism in the twentieth century, was in this way the principal avenue to black unity in antebellum America. Whether free black or slave, whether in the North or in the South, the ultimate impact of that development was profound. During the process of their becoming a single people, Yorubas, Akans, Ibos, Angolans, and others were present on slave ships to America and experienced a common horror—unearthly moans and piercing shrieks, the smell of filth and the stench of death, all during the violent rhythms and quiet coursings of ships at sea. As such, slave ships were the first real incubators of slave unity across cultural lines, cruelly revealing irreducible links from one ethnic group to the other, fostering resistance thousands of miles before the shores of the new land appeared on the horizon—before there was mention of natural rights in North America. (Stuckey, *op cit.*, p.1)

Cultural Integrity

Culture is the vehicle that moves all human groups forward; and to achieve its purpose an essential integrity must inhere in and guide the culture. Integrity unites correctness and wholeness. A culture must answer such questions as "What do we believe in?", "What behavior is acceptable, what honored, and what punished?", "How do we raise and educate our children?", and "What do we do best, which can be strategically utilized to support and sustain us, so that we can provide for our needs and live as we choose and decide to live?" The African American group lacks cultural integrity, and has started a process of self- correction and consensus-building for the explicit purpose of rectifying this very serious problem. In many important respects, our forbearers who were slaves,

sharecroppers, and servants enjoyed a higher degree of cultural integrity than we do today. They founded schools, busi-
nesses, and mutual aid societies together; their values and
their devotion to duty were rock steady; they made time to
help and care for one another and to enforce and pass on
their beliefs, intentions, ways of doing things, traditions and
group vision. They resisted systemic assaults on their dignity
and humanity; and they perpetuated and advanced our group.

One defining characteristic of the African American
group is its unyielding democratic spirit:

> It was the black man that raised a vision of democracy in America
> such as neither Americans nor Europeans conceived in the eigh-
> teenth century and such as they have not conceived in the twen-
> tieth century; and yet a conception which every clear sighted
> man knows is true and inevitable. One cannot think then of
> democracy in America or in the modern world without refer-
> ence of the American Negro. The democracy established in
> America in the eighteenth century was not, and was not designed
> to be, a democracy of the masses of men and it was thus singu-
> larly easy for people to fail to see the incongruity of democracy
> and slavery. It was the Negro himself who forced the consider-
> ation of this incongruity, who made emancipation inevitable and
> made the modern world at least consider if not wholly accept
> the idea of a democracy including men of all races and colors.
> W. E. B. Du Bois, *The Gift of Black Folk; Negroes in the Making
> of America*, (Boston: Stratford Company, 1924), pp. 66–67.

Continuing and expanding this historic role as definers
and enforcers of democracy is a crucial component of the
African American cultural offensive now underway.

Yet, vigilance with respect to external challenges must
not prevent our group from looking inward for the purpose
of self- and group-development, however difficult it is to attend to all the urgent priorities which must be met. Today,
our young people are asking the most troubling questions that
can be asked of a culture: "What difference does it make
whether I live or die; whether I learn anything in school; or

become an addict, a criminal or a murderer?" The culture must answer these questions in one clear, strong voice.

The African American cultural offensive will certainly fail if it lacks the will to unify leadership and resources around the issues which today decimate the children and young adults of our group. We have retrogressed to the point where half of our babies under six years old are officially in poverty. **Half of our babies.** Most of them are parented only by poor, isolated teen- aged girls. More of our young men are in prison than in college; and too many of those who have managed to steer clear of the law are nevertheless poorly educated, unemployed, underemployed, unwelcome in the labor force, and unable to assume the responsibilities of marriage and family life. Though the African American community told the nation that heavily addictive drugs were being imported into our communities, particularly victimizing our young before they knew what was happening to them nearly fifty years ago, and the nation did not respond so long as the problem was confined to our communities. Still we must ourselves overturn and drive out the drug subculture that now infests our neighborhoods. The culture must not stand by and watch these tragedies play themselves out; it must step in. It must create the environment which fosters and nurtures a radically different self- perception and sense of possibility than the one most of our children now know. It must remember that it teaches best not pedantically, or nostalgically, by castigation or by attempts at intimidation across class lines or generation gaps, but by example.

Education

Education is the key which unlocks both the door to group advancement and the door into the American economic mainstream; but the education that most African American students receive most often turns out to be a defective key which fails to open either door. Why are so many of our children geniuses in the streets and functional illiterates in classrooms, test sites, and personnel offices? One reason is that the legacy of enslavement, with its enforcement and security arms of systemic poverty and ignorance, continues to keep the opportunity, human and financial resources and facilities of these students at a bare minimum. This is the main problem which school desegregation and integration policy sought to resolve. However, today many question what was gained and what was lost in the several compromise plans that constituted desegregation as it has been experienced in African American communities. This is a question which our culture should examine thoroughly.

African American educators have identified, tested and proven a number of successful philosophies and methods of creating effective learning environments. *We must be present at the tables where policy about the education of our children is made.* We know how to educate our children; but we are excluded from the decision-making processes. *We must stop this negative pathology approach which defines our children. "Permanent underclass," "at risk," "disadvantaged."* These are powerful, negative self-fulfilling prophesies; and we must stop ourselves, and stop permitting others to define our children in this way.

Effective learning environments begin with the highest expectations and vision of what our group and our children can be; they involve parents, families and the community intimately in their work; they are cooperative rather than competitive settings; and they utilize cultural studies, and hands-on, inquiry-based formats. The culture will want to study these approaches, assess their value in making the sort of paradigm shift which is necessary to authentically prepare our children for the workplace and the leadership required for the 21st Century, and then institutionalize such programs, system-wide, in both schools and community-based organizations and churches. I would like to show you a videotape at this time, which brings these messages together. It is a joint effort of the National Urban Coalition and SMART, entitled

"The New ABC's; Preparing Black Children for the 21st Century."

At the African American Summit '89, there was an overwhelming consensus around the need to establish a national commission within the group, to look at needs, effective strategies, an Afrocentric curriculum, and resource development for education. This commission would define and then work toward implementing a program of education designed to tap the genius of African American children, their families and teachers, and prepare them fully as productive group members and as citizens of the U.S. and of the global village. And I am pleased to be able to tell you that we are convening at Lincoln University this month, a special task force which will decide upon the appropriate curricula for our children, pre-K through senior high schools, which will be given to our people in cities and states around the nation. They want a curriculum they can insist be *mandatory* in our schools; and we are going to hold counsel with our best minds and give them that curriculum.

Given the demographics of the 1990's, the nation needs the success of these efforts to protect its own economic interests. Whether it will make the investments needed to secure a favorable outcome remains to be seen.

Now we hope that you will agree with us, that the point of making the paradigm shift we seek, that overturning European cultural hegemony by crafting African-centered curricula, that the point of this is not simply to train African people to do the same things that Europeans are now doing. The point is not simply to "get our piece of the pie"—the same pie that we now know. No! As we have said many times, in many contexts, once we get into the mainstream, *the mainstream will change.* And there is one kind of change in particular that I would like to close with today: **A change in the way we think, and teach students to think; a change in thinking itself.**

In ancient Egypt, which as you know was the center of much of our golden age that we can still access, the process of thinking itself was very different from that which the Europeans have developed and advanced. The Egyptians thought in terms of **symbols** rather than objects. Symbolism is an **intuitive** means of overcoming the limitations of brain-centered reason. Symbolism does not merely count what the five senses can detect, it creates a new relationship between **inner knowing** and external analysis. European objective, linear thought consciously excludes any relationship to the unseen, or spiritual, dimension of life. But in the Egyptian hieroglyphic writing, we receive a whole complex of abstract, intuitive states of being as well as material facts, which are not so much described, as **experienced** in symbolism, we see not the effects, but the cause; we experience non-polarized expressions of the will or the spirit, not mere sequential sense-reports based only in the limited perceptions of the human.

Let me show you an example of what I mean. Please turn to the page in our document, "Cultural Connections," where we find the eye of Horus [description is read from this page.]

So you see, the ancient Egyptians did not separate or divorce the spiritual from the scientific. They employed a **sacred science** which produced miracles of technological achievement which are still not understood today. And I submit to you that we cannot today move into a study of science with spiritual dimensions without a transformation of our thinking—away from the objectified, linear European mode and back to a symbolism which will teach us what our past holds for us, and lead us into the new millennium.

Special training and a self-conscious reorientation of our minds, and our habits and modalities of thinking, will be required if we are to progress, and to help all humanity to progress, in this direction of expanded consciousness and sacred science. I strongly urge all who are intrigued by this prospect to study the work of R. A. Schwaller de Lubicz, along with our own scholars of Egyptology such as Dr. Asa G. Hilliard, III, for this purpose. The implications for curricular changes and advances are enormous. Certainly we need the benefit of new insights into the creation and uses of technology which will help rather than destroy humankind. The redevelopment of sacred science will assure such benefits.

While we have much to do, the challenge is compelling—and even thrilling, if we see the potential mastery and power that are inherent in our being African in America. But let us never forget what the bottom-line stakes for us entail. Let us hear well the words of W. E. B. Dubois:

> This the American black man knows: his fight here is a fight to the finish. Either he does or wins. If he wins it will be by no subterfuge or evasion of amalgamation. He will enter modern civilization here in America a black man on terms of perfect and unlimited equality with any white man, or he will enter not at all. Either extermination root and branch, or absolute equality. There can be no compromise. This is the last great battle of the West. (*Black Reconstruction*, p. 703)

Let us stay together, and work together, until African and African American content is thoroughly infused into the school curricula of our children; until, through their great talent and genius, building on a solid foundation which we have helped to lay, perfect cultural equality and the advance of all humanity, are ours!

God bless Africa and her children throughout the earth.

SECTION II

HISTORY, ART, AND THE SPREAD OF AFRICAN PEOPLE IN THE WEST

History teaches us that, in certain circumstances, it is very easy for the foreigner to impose his domination on a people. But it also teaches us that, whatever may be the material aspects of this domination, it can be maintained only by the permanent, organized repression of the cultural life of the people concerned. Implantation of foreign domination can be assured definitely only by physical liquidation of a significant part of the dominated population.

In fact, to take up arms to dominate a people is, above all, to take up arms to destroy, or at least to neutralize, to paralyze, its cultural life.

—Amilcar Cabral

John Henrik Clarke, Ph.D.
Teacher, Historian, Writer, Lecturer, Reviewer

John Henrik Clarke is a unique resource and a special institution in the African World. Beginning with his early years, Dr. Clarke studied the world of African people and became a master teacher. Presently, he is a distinguished Professor Emeritus of African World History at Hunter College in New York City. He has also served as the Carter G. Woodson Distinguished Visiting Professor at the Africana Studies and Research Center, Cornell University. An eminent Africanist and historian, he is editor of 21 books and has written several others, as well as short stories and pamphlets on African and African-American History. Dr. Clarke, an international traveler and world-renowned lecturer, has delivered presentations throughout the United States and abroad.

African People on My Mind
BY JOHN HENRIK CLARKE

The title, "The Infusion of African and African-American Content in the School Curriculum," symbolizes a long conflict that was set in motion in the 16th century with the second rise of Europe and the start of the Atlantic slave trade and subsequently the colonial system. We could be more confident about the infusion of African and African-American content in the school curriculum if we were clear about how and why African people were originally removed from the respectful commentary of history in order to justify their enslavement and oppression.

Over the years I have spoken so often on the subject that I have exhausted most of my arguments. If it were my choice to speak directly on the subject, I would be obliged to speak for a week. If it were my choice to be thorough and speak in great detail on the subject, I could speak indefinitely. My approach to the subject matter is personal because the search for a definition of African people in world history has been one of the great obsessions of my life. My self, my style, my education and what I call my mission in life has been built around a serious study of this subject. This is a personal talk about my commitment as a teacher in relationship to this subject using the main currents in my own life, from a sharecropper farm in Alabama to becoming a teacher in New York City who made some original contributions to the field.

My search began when I was a Baptist Sunday School teacher and tried to find the image of my people in the Bible. When I did not see anyone in the illustrated copies of the Bible or the printed Sunday School lessons that looked like me or members of my family, I began to wonder how we were left out of this sacred book that is supposed to be the word of God. (At that time I did not know that the Sunday School lessons were printed by a white Baptist publishing company in Nashville, Tennessee). Most of the Bible unfolds in Africa, but there were no African people in the pictorial texts. When I wondered out loud who left us out of God's Holy Book, I was told to, "Shut-up," and that my questions were out of order. As a young man my problems in relationship to the Bible were multiplied when I saw the pictures of all those white angels and wondered out loud again that of all the Black, Brown and Yellow people in the world how come not one of them became an angel. I did not know, at that time, that my mind was being prepared not only to inquire into biblical history, but into history in general. It would be many years before I would read the literature on how the Bible was written, in other works on the formation of the world's religions.

As I grew into early manhood in Columbus, Georgia, I continued the search. When I asked a white lawyer that I worked for, before and after school, to lend me a book on African people in ancient history, he shook his head and smiled in sympathy and said in a gentle tone, "John, you come from a people who have no history." I heard his word, but could not accept the meaning of what he had said. While doing chores at Spencer High School in Columbus, I was told to watch the books and the coat of a recitalist who had come to the school to help raise funds for a curtain for the auditorium. While he was on stage, I opened one of his books that was entitled, "The New Negro." By some stroke of good fortune, the first essay I saw in the opened book was called, "The Negro Digs Up His Past" by Arthur Schomburg. From this essay I learned that I came from a people who had a long and honorable history, one that pre-dated the existence of Europe. This knowledge surged through my mind like a liberating force.

When I came to New York City, in 1933, I began my search for Arthur Schomburg. We met in the summer of 1934 and he remained one of my teachers until he died in 1938. Arthur Schomburg told me that what I was calling "Negro History" and "African History" was the missing pages of world history. He suggested that I should read European history in order to learn how African people were left out of world history. He repeatedly emphasized that no one can successfully oppress a consciously historical people. In order to oppress a people, he said, you must remove them from history and make them believe that the Gods of their creation are weak and unworthy. You must assign them to a god-concept created by the same people whose intention it is to rule them. In essence, Arthur Schomburg taught me the inter-relationship of African history to world history.

At The Harlem History Club, then functioning out of the Harlem YMCA, on 135th Street in Harlem, Dr. Willis N. Huggins, founder of the club, taught me the political meaning of history. By listening to the lectures of Professor William Leo Hansberry, of Howard University, I learned the philosophical meaning of history. My point here: I was trained by great Black master-teachers who only asked me to learn history well, and pass it on to others who need to know it.

Willis N. Huggins, with his brilliant young protege, John G. Jackson, wrote two pioneering books on Africa for the History Club, A *Guide to Studies in African History*, and *An Introduction to African Civilizations*. On his own, John G. Jackson had already written the pamphlet, *Was Jesus Christ a Negro?* and *The African Origin of the Myths and Legends of the Garden of Eden*. Jackson wold later write two other important pamphlets, *Pagan Origins of the Christ Myth* and *Christianity Before Christ*, his inquiry into the role of Ethiopia as the origin of the civilization that would later be called the Egyptian civilization.

As for African-American history, I had seriously studied Carter G. Woodson's monumental contribution, *The Negro in our History*, and his book on Africa, which is still worth reading, *The African Background Outlined*. In this field there were meaningful voices from the Caribbean Islands, the best known, J. A. Rogers of Jamaica, who spent most of his life explaining the role that African personalities have played in world history. His best known work on the subject is *World's Great Men of Color*, Volumes I and II, originally published in 1946 and reprinted in 1972 by MacMillan and Company. Raphael Powell had already written, *The Human Side of a People and the Right Name*. This is the first book that challenged the use of the word, "Negro."

Our interest in Africa was stimulated, with some sadness, by the Italian-Ethiopian War. Ethiopia's tragic defeat made a lot of us look at ourselves as an African people under siege. Willis N. Huggins had gone to Geneva to hear the League of Nation's debate about the Ethiopian situation. In his absence, John Jackson and I took over the leadership of the Harlem History Club temporarily. John Jackson's first lecture was "The Black Man as an Imperialist." It dealt with a subject that is still unknown to most students interested in Africa. I delivered the second lecture. My subject was "An Inquiry Into the Racial Identity of Jesus Christ." Later I extended the idea into a short story that has been reprinted in anthologies throughout the world. The story is entitled, "The Boy Who Painted Christ Black."

By the time of the death of Willis N. Huggins, in 1939, the Harlem History Club had gone through a number of changes. It was now called The Blyden Society, after Edward Wilmot Blyden, the great Caribbean patriot who had gone to Africa in the 1850's from the Virgin Islands. The Harlem History Club had been an informal university. Most subjects relating to African people throughout the world were taught there. For a brief period, one of the members of the club was a very studious African from the Gold Coast, now called Ghana. At the time he was referred to as Francis K. Nkrumah. We did not know, at the time, that he would eventually head an independent state in Africa under the name of Kwame Nkrumah.

John G. Jackson continued to write pamphlets and I continued to write poetry and short stories. By a careful selection of books from second-hand bookstores, I gave myself an informal high school education and began the study of college textbooks. Using this method of study I had more than the equivalent of a college education.

After being discharged from the Army in 1945, I attended New York University under the G.I. Bill of Rights. There I discovered that I knew more about history and some general subjects than most of my teachers. My first experience in teaching African history was in the Harlem community, in churches and community centers. The members of the once well-attended Harlem History Club had scattered now and a few of them had died. John G. Jackson and I remained friends. Both of us were rediscovered in the 50's after the Supreme Court's decision outlawing school segregation, in 1954, and the Montgomery Bus Boycott in 1955. African-Americans in increasing numbers were demanding to know their place in history. Most of the answers, and some of the documented information, was now coming from informally-trained historians like John G. Jackson, Joel A. Rogers, myself and a number of others. In a marginal way, we were finally getting some of the attention we needed.

I continued to write an occasional article on an African subject for African-American newspapers and some small white literary journals. I wrote a number of books that did not interest any publishers, and I did not have the funds to publish the books myself. At this time I had only one published book to my credit, a book of poetry, *Rebellion in Rhyme*, published in 1948 by a small publishing house in Indiana. I attended a clinic for professional writers at New York University and wrote several books as a class exercise. The most meaningful book was *Journey to the Fair*, a semi-autobiographical novel about a 17-year-old Black youngster hoboing across the United States and ending up at the Chicago World's Fair of 1933. The novel was never published because it was about the world of the vagabonds of America, where there is very little emphasis placed on race. Most publishers liked the book, but told me finally that they could not sell a non- racial book in a racist society. I continued to write books whether anyone cared to publish them or not.

My research into African resistance movements that were led by African kings resulted in a book named *Lives of Great African Chiefs*. This book was published in newspaper serial form in the *Pittsburgh Courier*, in 1957 and 1958. Some of these installments were reprinted in newspapers in Africa. This gave me the reading audience I wanted and needed, although it gave me not much money of consequence.

In the summer of 1958, after many years of longing to do so, I made my first trip to Africa. I visited Ghana the second year after its independence. In all of Africa there was no better place to be this time in history. I found the Ghanaians to be a beautiful people, full of self-confidence, proud of their newly proclaimed nationhood and their president. I did not go to Africa as a tourist. I lived with the people, in the slums of the city of Accra, sharing the one-room apartment of a Ghanaian whom I had met through a long pen-pal relationship. His name was James Kotey. For a while I worked as a reporter for Nkrumah's newspaper, *The Evening News*, under one of the most remarkable editors—his name was Eric Hyman. In Africa I felt that I had found my place in the world. I did not know it at the time, but I wold visit different parts of Africa three times a year for the next 20 years.

On my way home from this first visit to Africa, I stopped in Rome to attend a meeting of the American Society for African Culture sponsored by the International Society of African Culture. This meeting in Rome was postponed in favor of a preparatory meeting in Paris. The purpose of the preparatory meeting was to prepare the agenda for the Second International Congress of Black Writers. So I went on to Paris. In Paris I was fortunate to meet the editor of *Presence Africaine*, Alioune Diop, and a large number of French-speaking Africans then residing in Paris, such as Rene Moran and others.

I was keeping notes on my African trip with the hope that I would write an acceptable book. The first of the many articles that I would write for the magazine *Presence Africaine*, was written during this trip. It was called, "Wake Keeping." It told the story of the celebration of a wake among the Ga people of Ghana. Over the next 30 years I would contribute more articles to *Presence Africaine* than all the writers in the United States combined. This was the beginning of my relationship with the Francophone African community. My acquaintance with this community would lead to my meeting with Cheikh Anta Diop during the Second International Congress of Africanists, held in Dakar, Senegal. Our friendship began during this meeting and lasted until his death. I believed deeply in this man and his work and respected him as a colleague and as a brother. It is a fact known by very few, but I, singularly, was responsible for his work being published in this country.

After the publication of his work, *African Origins of Civilization: Myth or Reality*, three more of Diop's works were published in the United States. They are: *Pre-Colonial Black Africa*, and *Black Africa: The Economic and Cultural Basis for a Federated State*, and *The Cultural Unity of Black Africa*. His last book will be published posthumously in the United States this fall. It is entitled, *Civilization or Barbarism*. All of his books except *The Cultural Unity of Black Africa* were published by Lawrence Hill and Company of Westport, Connecticut. *The Cultural Unity of Black Africa* was published by the Third World Press of Chicago, Illinois.

When I arrived back in this country, in 1958, after my first trip to Africa, I decided that I would write and devote the rest of my life to writing, research, and teaching about Africa and African people all over the world. My noble pursuit of this goal drove me to the brink of starvation and I still would not give up. In 1961 I became an associate editor for the magazine *Freedomways*, where I remained for 21 years. I conceived and edited the first African issue of this magazine and most of the special issues, including the special Harlem issue and special issues on the lives of Paul Robeson and Dr. W. E. B. DuBois. *Freedomways* paid very little and I now had a family to support. I worked at many other jobs. For five years I was director of the Heritage Teaching Program of the Anti-Poverty Program in Harlem. Here I began to develop study guides on African and African-American history. I later, taught at New York University's Headstart Program and in the African Studies Center at their New School for Social Research. For the next 10 years I had as much work as I had the time and the energy to do. My articles and conference papers on Africa and African history were now appearing in leading journals throughout the world. I edited three books on the Harlem community that all sold well. Over the years I would edit 21 books, including the first anthology of short stories by Black writers.

In 1967 I attended a meeting of the African Studies Association in Los Angeles and joined other Black scholars who challenged the interpretation of African history by paternalistic white scholars. This challenge eventually led to the establishment of the African Heritage Studies Association and my election to head it as its first president. I was hired to teach African-American history at Hunter College the same year. When I was asked about my degree, I said, "Show me a classroom and some students and I will demonstrate my degree." I did this very effectively for nearly 20 years. I retired from teaching in the spring of 1988, due mainly to a sight deficiency brought on by glaucoma.

I continue to write, travel, and lecture throughout the country and abroad. I have finished four books and have visited Africa four times since being declared legally blind. I have recently completed a book called, *The African World at the Crossroads*. In this book I raised the questions, "What happened to African people in the second half of the 20th century?" and "What happened to the bright promise reflected in the African Independence Explosion, the American Civil Rights Movement, and the idea of a Caribbean Federation?" As we African people face the 21st Century, there might be as many as a billion of us on this earth. How can we still answer to the name, "minority?" Why do so many of us have a self-concept assigned to us by other people? More critically, why do so many of us have a God-concept assigned to us by other people? We are an African people wherever we are on the face of this earth! Why are so many of us afraid to face this fact? No people can be whole without an understanding of their history and this understanding must begin with a definition of their history.

To me history is the clock that people use to tell their political and cultural time of day. It is also a clock that they use to find themselves on the map of human geography. The role of history in the final analysis is to tell a people where they have been and what they have been, where they are and what they are. Most importantly, the role of history is to tell a people where they still must go and what they still must be. To me the relationship of a people to their history is the same as the relationship of a child to its mother.

Despite centuries of textbook distortions and omissions, there is a new wave of academic rebellion spreading across this country. A resurgence of cultural pride is manifested in the variety of demands being made for curriculum revision.

(Harold E. Charles, *Chicago Defender*, July 29, 1989)

Robert Farris Thompson, Ph.D.
Professor, History of Art and African Studies
Master of Timothy Dwight College
Yale University

Dr. Thompson organized the 1981 exhibition at the National Gallery of Art entitled, "The Four Moments of the Sun," and is working on a second, "The Face of the Gods: Art and Altars of the Black Atlantic World," scheduled for 1991. He served as consultant and moderator for the BBC documentary film, "Secret African City," which aired earlier this year. Dr. Thompson has written numerous articles and several books, the most recent of which is *Flash of the Spirit*. He earned bachelor's, master's and doctoral degrees at Yale.

African Survivals in the Black Atlantic World
BY ROBERT FARRIS THOMPSON

Edited Excerpts

In a captivating slide lecture presentation Dr. Robert Farris Thompson documented various aspects of African cultural survivals often overlooked or neglected in teaching African American history and culture. These survivals were traced through the disciplines of Art, Music, Religion, the Martial Arts, Language, and History. To recapture the essential message of the presentation given extemporaneously, excerpts from previously published material by Dr. Thompson are quoted extensively. Curriculum specialists were especially encouraged to research, document and study these various cultural retentions by African Americans. A highlight of the lecture was the emphasis on the diverse presence of people of African descent throughout the Black Atlantic World in Brazil, Cuba, North America, and the Caribbean. In the article, *Black Ideographic Writing: Calabar to Cuba*, Thompson records cultural retentions still present in the heritage of African Americans:

> . . . classical elements of African Art and culture were brought from Nigeria to Brazil; Dahomey and Kongo to Haiti; Kongo and the Bight of Biafra to North America; Mali to the southwest coast of Mexico...the visual influence of tropical Africa upon the peoples of the Americas constitutes a parallel classical civilization, bound to rational orders simultaneously embodying spontaneity and decorum and responding to the imperatives of life. "Classical" is a strong word to apply to a continent of people who everyone assumes could not read or write before the coming of the nineteenth-century colonialists and missionaries. But the

truth is that —not even considering Muslim black civilizations of the Sudan in which clerical figures had been writing African languages in Arabic script since medieval times—several African civilizations (e.g., the Mande of modern Mali, the Ejagham of western Cameroon and adjacent Nigeria, and the Bakongo of Bas-Zaire and Northern Angola) had independently elaborated complex systems of ideographic signs prior to colonial times. What is more, some of these signs were remembered and developed, even under conditions of slavery, by blacks in the Americas. Blazons and ideographs were carefully guarded by priests and other important figures in the African-derived cult life of several cities of the Western Hemisphere, notably Havana, Rio de Janeiro, and Port-au-Prince. . . . Calabar captives brought nsibidi signs to that portion of the New World where they were most heavily concentrated in the nineteenth century, the sugar ports of western Cuba, primarily Cardenas, Matanzas, and Havana. In the process, a linked African and Afro-American classical tradition was established, a strong cultural assertion binding together Cuba and Calabar, creating an animating power equal to the challenges of its shifting historical situation.

Thompson graphically through visuals illustrated the influence of Africa in the Art of African Americans. Writing in the essay, *"African Influence on the Art of the United States"* (1981) in the *Journal of African Civilizations,* Thompson stated:

"Present to this day are African influenced verbal arts (Aunt Nancy tales), healing (conjuring), cuisine (hog maws and collard greens), singing (field hollers and work songs), and dance forms in considerable quantity. And present, too, are parallel visual continuities: amazing stoneware vessels shaped in the form of anguished human faces made by Afro-Americans in South Carolina in the last century, multiple wood carving modes in Tidewater, Georgia, basketry modes of astonishing purity near Charleston, the deliberate decoration of graves in the African manner with surface deposits of broken earthenware and possessions in many parts of the Deep South, and isolated instances of Afro-American wood carving in Livingston County, Missouri, and Onondaga County, New York...By the hand of individual Afro-American masters were fashioned works of art whose blending

of remembered ancestral and encountered alien modes may now
be estimated and explored."

The African influence on the Music of the Americas was
given detailed expression; Thompson spoke to the issue in
stating:

"Here one learns that the basic structural traits which define
West Africa as a province in world music (dominance of a percus-
sive concept of music, off-beat phrasing of melodic accents, over-
lapping of vocal and instrumental patterns of call and response,
and so forth) reappear in United States Afro-American musical
forms such as the work song and the ring shout. These musical
continuities are so visible and massive that they cannot by any
stretch of the imagination be characterized as esoteric or circum-
stantial, and they demolish by virtue of existence the new myth
of the disappearance of the Afro-American's past in the United
States. Indeed, from the further development of the work song
and the ring shout have arisen the basic cafe musics of the world
in the twentieth century. The triumph of jazz and the blues
indicates that something is wrong somewhere with the theory of
slaves rejecting their meaningless past for the cultural standards
of their master. This does not mean that there was no borrowing
from Western music and other cultural forms, but jazz and the
blues do not sound like weakened European folk music precisely
because their innovators respected African traditions of timing,
timbre, and so forth, which had not in the least been forgotten
or jettisoned."

As a special appeal Dr. Robert Farris Thompson documented the origin and development of the martial art form,
Capoeira. Through various slides and historical information
the profound influence of Africans in Brazil towards its development were given detailed emphasis. Bira Almeida in his
excellent history of Capoeira, *Capoeira: A Brazilian Art Form,
History, Philosophy, and Practice*, records its development
thusly:

In spite of the oppression, the Africans and their descendants
developed an extraordinary cultural, social, and political universe

parallel to the social system imposed on them, keeping alive many expressions of African culture, some of them traditionally preserved, others gradually assuming new forms. Perhaps Capoeira is one of these expressions, or at least, a consequence of this process.

There are many theories about the origin of Capoeira. One of the most popular among young contemporary capoeiristas is presented by Augusta Ferreira who emphasizes the martial aspects of the art.

Capoeira was born out of the burning desire for freedom. Only through the efforts of these men would the slaves free themselves, and return once more to the life of freedom they had known in their own land. The first steps toward this reconquest of freedom were taken when the Dutch lashed out at the Portuguese Colony, invading the towns and plantations along the Northeastern Coast concentrating on Recife and Salvador. With each Dutch invasion the security systems of the plantations and towns were weakened and the slaves, taking advantage of the opportunities, fled, plunging into the forests in search of safe places in which to hide and survive...

At the time the land along the coast was separated from the interior lands by a strip of Amazon-type forest, traces of which are still found today. It was in this strip of forest, in areas 100 kilometers wide, that the best hiding places were found. These areas were known as capoeiras. The process of isolation and fortification caused the fugitive blacks to develop a system for freeing the slaves still captive on the plantations and in the towns...

Capoeira developed its structure as a fight in the quilombos. The embryo of capoeira as a rudimentary fighting style was created in the slaves' quarters and perhaps would not have developed further if left only to that environment. It would have been only a series of strike movements, utilizing above all the muscular strength of its practitioners. It would have remained an essentially rustic style used only to evade the aggressions of the slaves' captors and masters. The development of capoeira as a fight occurred in the quilombos, basically because it was needed not just to defend against physical aggression, but as a defense in life or death situations in which the attackers did not simply use whips, but rather deadly weapons, even firearms and cannon...

Another indication that capoeira was used by people of Palmares was its diffusion throughout large parts of Brazil. When the quilombos were destroyed, the watchful warriors, no longer able to stay together, were scattered throughout several states, even as far as Rio Grande do Sul, and with them their fight, traced to them through studies in following centuries.

In his lecture Dr. Thompson rendered a bio-sketch of Mestre Bimba, one of the African diasporan founders of capoeira. Bira Almeida presents the following historical biography of Mestre Bimba:

> Bimba (Manoel dos Reis Machado) was born on November 23, 1899, in Salvador, capital of the Bahia state. He earned his nickname from a bet between his mother, Maria Martinha do Bonfim and the midwife who delivered him—bimba is a popular term for a male child's sexual organ in Bahia. He began to learn Capoeira at the age of 12, with Bentinho, an African who was a boat commander for the coastwise navigation company within the Bay of All Saints.
>
> The importance of Mestra Bimba in the history of Capoeira was definitively established when he became the first mestre to open a formal school of Capoeira in 1932. On July 9, 1937, the course of Capoeira history changed with the official recognition of his school by the government through the Office of Education and Public Assistance.
>
> Because of his effectiveness as a teacher and fighter, Mestre Bimba attracted many students who supported his goal of organizing a disciplined method of teaching and ultimately his efforts to legitimize Capoeira as a form of self-defense and an athletic game. He developed the style called Capoeira regional, improving the technical quality of movements taught—creating sequences of training, and enriching his contemporary Capoeira with sweeps from batuque, a rough kind of dance-fight that he learned from his father, the famous batuqueiro Luiz Candido Machado.

The richness of information of African cultural retentions by Blacks in the Atlantic World was attested to by Dr. Thompson as related stories of Anansi still told to African American children by their grandparents even today. Allen Counter and David Evans record this legacy in their splendid book, *I Sought My Brother: An Afro-American Reunion* (1981):

> An Africanism that has been with the bush people since their

ancestors brought it across the Atlantic is the Anansi Toree spider tales. These stories, told mainly to children and young teenagers, are always about Anansi, a clever, crafty spider who manages to outwit wrong-doers. The stories always carry a strong moral which helps teach cultural values to the young. Special adults in the village, usually men or older volunteers, are charged with telling Anansi Toree to the young who delight in hearing them. Usually in the quiet of dusk or early evening, children gather at a predesignated spot, generally the storyteller arrives to greet the group and make a few stories are told, some evoking laughter, others causing distress or sadness, but each carrying some precept for the ethical development of the young people (p. 129).

The profoundly diverse cultural heritage of African Americans has placed it in its proper perspective of a people's history that is wholistic, comprehensive and thematic. Dr. Robert Farris Thompson documents an essentially neglected fact that the history of peoples of African descent is richly intertwined with that of the cultures of the world whether they be in the Americas, north or south, the Caribbean, Europe, Asia or the Pacific Isles. It is this record that curriculum specialists and textbook authors must partake of in order to fully understand and appreciate the history of African and African American people.

To further efforts for educators to gain access to material in the areas on which Dr. Thompson concentrated his presentation, the editors offer the bibliography that follows.

BIBLIOGRAPHY

Alleyne, Mervyn C. (1980) *Comparative Afro-American: An Historical Comparative Study of English Based Afro-American Dialects of the New World.* Ann Arbor: Karoma Publishers.

Almeida, Bira (1986) *Capoeira: A Brazilian Art Form: History, Philosophy and Practice.* Berkeley: North Atlantic Books.

Andrews, George Reid (1979) "The Afro-Argentine Officers

of Buenos Aires Province, 1800-1860," *Journal of Negro History*, 64, Spring, pp. 85-100.

Andrews, George Reid (1979) "Race Versus Class Association: The Afro-Argentines of Buenos Aires, 1850-1900." *Journal of Latin American Studies*, 11, May, pp. 19-39.

Andrews, George Reid (1980) *The Afro-Argentines of Buenos Aires 1800-1900*. Wisconsin: The University of Wisconsin Press.

Bastide, Roger (1971) *African Civilizations in the New World*. New York: Harper Torch Books.

Burns, E. Bradford (1974) "Manuel Querino's Interpretation of the African Contribution to Brazil," *Journal of Negro History*, Vol. LIX, No. 1, January, pp. 78-86.

Calomee, Gloria (1986) "A Crisis Report on Brazil and Blacks of South America," *Crisis*, June/July, pp. 37-40, 58-64.

Counter, A. and Evans, D. L. (1981) *I Sought My Brother: An Afro-American Reunion*. Cambridge: MIT Press.

Cortada, Rafael L. (1970) "The African Diaspora: The Black Man in the Development of South America." *A Current Bibliography on African Affairs*, October, pp. 5-20.

Dilorenzo, Kris (1986) "A Crisis Report on the Blacks of Central America," *Crisis*, June/July, pp. 29-34, 60-61.

Fermeselle-Lopez, Rafael (1972) "Black Politics in Cuba: The Race War of 1912." Ph.D. Dissertation, American University.

Fikes, Robert, Jr. (1984-84) "Blacks in Europe, Asia, Canada, and Latin America: A Bibliographical Essay," *A Current Bibliography on African Affairs*, Vol. 17(2), pp. 113-128.

Glasgow, Roy Arthur (1975) "Afro-Latinos: Presence and Impact." *National Scene Family News Supplement*, Vol. IV, No. 3, June/July, pp. 3-5.

Hawkins, Odie (1984) "Capoeira: Combat as Art: Brazil's Martial Tradition," *Players Magazine*, Vol. 10, No. 8, pp. 28-29, 62-63.

Irwin, Graham W. (1977) *Africans Abroad: A Documentary History of the Black Diaspora in Asia, Latin America, and the Caribbean During the Age of Slavery*. New York: Columbia University Press.

Kennedy, James H. (1984-85) "Recent Afro-Brazilian Literature: A Tentative Bibliography," A *Current Bibliography on African Affairs*. Vol. 17, No. 4, pp. 327-345.

Kent, R. K. (1965) "Palmares: An African State in Brazil," *Journal of African History*, 6, pp. 169-75.

Kipples, Kenneth F. (1976) *Blacks in Colonial Cuba 1774-1899*. Gainesville, Fla.

Marshall, Bernard (1975) "The Black Caribs-Native Resistance to British Penetration into the Windward Side of St. Vincent 1763-1773," *Pan-African Journal*, Vol. VIII, No. 2, Summer, pp. 139-152.

Martin, Tony (1975) "Repression and Resistance in West Indian History," *Pan-African Journal*, Vol. VIII, No. 2, Summer, pp. 125-138.

Nascimento, Elisa Larkin (1930) *Pan-Africanism and South America: Emergence of a Black Rebellion*. Buffalo: Afrodiaspora.

Pierson, Donald (1942) *Negroes In Brazil: A Study of Race Contact at Bahia*. Chicago: University of Chicago Press.

Price, Richard (1983) *To Slay the Hydra: Dutch Colonial Perspectives on the Saramaka Wars*. Ann Arbor: Karoma Publishers, Inc.

Price, Richard (1983) *First Time: The Historical Vision of an Afro-American People*. London: John Hopkins University Press.

Price, Richard (1976) *The Guiana Maroons: A Historical and Bibliographical Introduction*. London: John Hopkins University Press.

Ramos, Arthur (1939) *The Negro in Brazil*. Washington, D.C.: Associated Publishers.

Rout, L. B. (1976) *The African Experience in Spanish America 1502 to the Present Day*. New York: Cambridge.

Saakana, Amon Saba (1983) "Carlos Moore on Blacks in Cuba: An Interview," *Frontline*, Sept./Oct., Vol. 2, No. 5, pp. 119-123.

Salaam, Yusef A. (1977) *The African/Bilalian and the Martial Arts: The Black Man's Contribution to the Fighting Arts.* New York: African/Bilalian Publications.

Sater, William F. (1974) "The Black Experience in Chile," In Robert Brent Toplin (Ed.) *Slavery and Race Relations in Latin American.* Westport: pp. 21–22.

Thompson, Era Bell (1974) "Argentina: Land of the Vanishing Blacks," *Ebony,* October, pp. 74–84.

Thompson, Robert Farris (1983) *Flash of the Spirit: African and Afro-American Art and Philosophy.* New York: Random House.

Thompson, Robert Farris (1973) "Yoruba Artistic Criticism," in Warren D'Azeriedo (Ed.) *The Traditional Artist in African Societies.* Bloomington: Indiana University Press, pp. 26, 60.

Thompson, Robert Farris (1974) *African Art in Motion.* Los Angeles: University of California Press.

Thompson, Robert Farris (1978) "Black Ideographic Writing: Calabar to Cuba," *Yale Alumni Magazine,* November, pp. 29–33.

Thompson, Robert Farris (1978) "The Flash of the Spirit: Haiti's Africanizing Voodun Art," in Ute Stebich, *Haitian Art,* New York: Abrams, pp. 34–35.

Thompson, Robert Farris (1981) "African Influence on the Art of the United States," in Ivan van Sertima (Ed.) *Journal of African Civilizations.* pp. 44–48.

Thompson, Robert Farris (N.D.) "Icons of the Mind: Yoruba Herbalism Arts in Atlantic Perspective" *African Arts* VIII, 3: pp. 52–59, 89–90.

Thompson, Robert Farris (N.D.) "The Face of the Gods: Art and Altars in the Black Atlantic World," Unpublished M.S. Thesis.

Turnbull, Colin M. (1977) "Bush Negroes Carry on Tradition of Rebel Ancestors," *Smithsonian,* Vol. 7, No. 12, pp. 78–85.

Turner, Lorenzo (1969) *Africanisms in the Gullah Dialect.* New York: Arno Press.

Vass, Winifred K. (1979) *The Bantu Speaking Heritage of the United States*. California: Center for Afro-American Studies.

Heritage, in essence, is the means by which people have used their talents to create a history that gives them memories they can respect and that they can use to command the respect of other people. The ultimate purpose of heritage and heritage teaching is to use people's talents to develop awareness and pride in themselves so that they themselves can achieve good relationships with other people.

—John Henrik Clarke

Richard A. Long, Ph.D.
Atticus Haygood Professor
of Interdisciplinary Studies
Emory University

Among his various achievements, Dr. Long is particularly noted for having conducted for 10 years at Atlanta University a series
of disciplinary Conferences on African and African-American
Studies. He is also the founder of the Triennial Symposium on
African Art, the Seventh Annual Meeting of which was conducted
in June of 1989 at the Smithsonian National Museum of African
Art. Dr. Long earned his bachelor's and master's degrees in English at Temple University. He holds a doctorate in Medieval Literature from the University of Poiters in France.

The African Diaspora
BY RICHARD A. LONG

It has only been during the last two decades that the term *African Diaspora* has been generally used to refer to the communities of people of Black African descent, scattered throughout the Western Hemisphere. The term at once expresses commonality with Africa as a place of origin and a distinction from Africa in time and place. The concept of the African Diaspora is the heir of the concept of Pan Africanism, first clearly articulated at the dawn of the century and equally the heir of the concept of Negritude, first clearly articulated in the thirties in this century. I stress "clearly articulated" since both Pan Africanism and Negritude have complex prehistories in the thought of such men as Edward Wilmot Blyden, George Washington Williams and Alexander Crommell.

The Pan African concept was chiefly political in its focus. Negritude was chiefly cultural. The concept of the African Diaspora, still emerging, subsumes these while emphasizing a historical dimension.

Diasporas have occurred throughout human history. The term itself, from a Greek word meaning dispersion or scattering, was first used in the Hellenistic Age to describe the dispersion of the Jews from Palestine during and after the Babylonian captivity. Until the 20th Century the term in fact denoted dispersion of the Jews. The term as used today requires some refinement. A "diasporic community" is a fact of history. The making of such a community, however, requires specification. Not only as to its place of origin but also as to its manner of creation. An open and free migration of people as, for example, that of the English, beginning in the 16th century, is one variety. Another variety is a refugee migration, motivated by political, military or economic circumstances such as that of the Vietnamese at present.

A third variety is a forced or coerced movement in which the intentions and will of the migrants are not taken into account. It was in this latter fashion that the African Diaspora in the Western Hemisphere was formed. This statement, however, requires modification and refinement by the recognition of the existence of primary, secondary and even further recessive diasporas.

Thus, at the beginning of the 20th century a secondary diaspora was created by West Indians, chiefly Jamaicans and Barbadians, who came to Panama to work on the construction of the canal and who remained in the new environment, joining in but not fusing with an older diasporic community in the country.

Thus, within the United States, African-Americans left the South in a continuous stream, beginning after the Civil War, to resettle in the North and in the Mid-West.

The dispersion of Black people from Sub-Saharan Africa has an extensive history. Their presence is attested in ancient Greece and Rome and later throughout the Islamic world. The mode of dispersion was by the caravan routes of the Sahara Desert and from the East Coast of Africa over the Pacific and its sub-bodies such as the Red Sea and the Indian Ocean.

The Trans-Saharans were well attested in Southern Europe, Italy, Iberia and Byzantium in the centuries preceding the Maritime Age but these dispersed peoples never formed diasporic communities. Chiefly functioning as domestic slaves, they interacted and interbred with bonded and other low status people, both native and alien, in the lands they inhabited and thus disappeared in a literal melting pot.

It is with the Maritime Age and more particularly the European colonization of the Western Hemisphere and the subsequent development of plantation society, the diasporic communities of the Western Hemisphere came into being. Using a hemispheric perspective we may divide the larger history of these communities into four periods: (1) the Maritime Age from about 1500 to 1600; (2) the First Plantation Age from about 1600 to 1800; (3) the Second Plantation Age from 1800 to 1890; and (4) the Modern Age from 1890 to the present. A rapid characterization of these periods may now be made.

During the Maritime Age, roughly co-extensive with the 16th Century, we witnessed the implantation of European colonies primarily in parts of the Caribbean and in Mexico, Central and South America, in brief, the Iberian implantation. The major colonial enterprise was the rapid acquisition of wealth particularly by the mining of precious metals. In portions of this colonial establishment, notably Mexico and Peru, there was in place a large industrious servile indigenous population which required little supplementation. In other areas such as in the Caribbean and Brazil the indigenous population lacked these qualities. The importation of African slave labor went therefore largely to the Caribbean and Brazil and only to a lesser degree to Mexico and Peru.

It is likely, however, that the Africans imported into the Western Hemisphere during the Maritime Age formed only transient diasporic communities and never attained the critical mass to continue to the present day. In other words no present day diasporic community can be reliably traced back to the 16th Century.

The First Plantation Age which may in fact be subdivided in a number of ways is that broad period of two centuries in which the slave trade dominates Atlantic commerce. Its end is marked by colonial revolt and rebellion and the rise of humanitarian concerns about the trade and about Slavery itself. At the beginning of that period we have the rapid entrance of English, Dutch and French colonial enterprise in the Western Hemisphere challenging Iberian sincerity and seizing land wherever possible.

Plantation agriculture becomes the chief economic activity and the production of sugar, tobacco, rice and indigo becomes the dominant concerns. The labor requirement of the plantation economy was enormous. In this period of two centuries approximately seven million and a half Africans arrived in the Americas. It is in the plantation societies, constituted by this vast migration that we can trace the origins of today's diasporic communities.

The Second Plantation Age, roughly co-extensive with the 19th Century, saw the cutting of political ties between Europe and the Euro-American colonies, leaving only the Caribbean, Canada and a few circum-Caribbean enclaves with continuing European political dependency.

The Second Plantation Age also saw increased profitability of plantation agriculture with the mechanization of cotton production in the United States and of sugar production in several places.

The increased labor needs of this new production, contending with heightened pressures against the Slave Trade and Slavery, resulted in tensions, crisis and in the United States Civil War. It is noteworthy that approximately two million more Africans enter the Western Hemisphere during this period. The abolition of slavery proceeded throughout this period beginning with the Haitian Revolution of the 1790s and ending with the final emancipation in Brazil in 1888, only 100 years ago. With some prudence it may be asserted that by the early years of the Second Plantation Age the basic elements of the diasporic communities we know today were in place.

Following a geographic scheme we may note the diasporic communities which are found today in the Western Hemisphere and place these under the rubric of the Modern Age. North America comprises Canada, the United States and, to the surprise of many, Mexico.

Canada's diasporic communities are secondary, small, fragile and diverse in origin. The earliest significant one is that of Nova Scotia which dates back to the end of the American Revolution. A later community developed from the Underground Railroad. The mid–20th Century saw migrations from the English-speaking Caribbean and from Haiti respectively to English and French- speaking areas of the Commonwealth.

The United States possesses, in addition to its large original primary diasporic communities, a secondary internal diaspora, a secondary diaspora from all regions of the Caribbean as well as a new primary diaspora from various parts of the African continent.

In Mexico there exists only relic diasporic communities, hardly known to the literature and to the Mexicans themselves. If you ask most Mexicans if there are Black people in Mexico they will say NO!! There are, but the communities are so small that you can forgive them for not knowing.

The complex case of Panama and Central America has already been referred to. The Caribbean coast of Central America, including Nicaragua and Costa Rica possess small secondary diaspora. Belize in Central America and the Guyanas in South America should be considered, for historical reasons, along with the Caribbean. Taking the total area of the Caribbean, which includes a variety of different societies and political arrangements, as well as a complex language situation, it is possible to describe its vast population as overwhelmingly of African descent.

So Euro-centric, however, are its traditional attitudes and understandings that generalizations about its diasporic communities are risky. Suffice it to say that the Hispanic areas, Cuba, Puerto Rico and the Dominican Republic differ significantly from the others for a variety of historical, cultural and demographic reasons. We might say that these communities all consider themselves to be white and in varying degrees are.

Columbia and Ecuador in South America have large diasporic populations while Peru, Chile, Paraguay and Uruguay have quite small ones, but some nevertheless. The largest countries of South America, Argentine and Brazil, offer contrasting situations. Both adapted, in the 19th Century, conscious "whitening" policies in order to reduce the percentage of people of African descent in their populations.

Temperate zones, sparsely populated Argentina with a relatively small Black population succeeded well, so much so that again Argentina is one of those places where they do not have any Black people. If you see Black people there they tell you, 'They just came over from Brazil.'

The modern diasporic community in Argentina is indeed small and is practically unknown to most Argentinians. Tropical plantation society, Brazil, had a relative success. While the diasporic population there is perhaps equal in size to or greater than that of the United States, it is powerless, poverty stricken and unthreatening.

Up to this point we have defined and described the Western Hemisphere Diaspora from Black Africa in broad terms. I would repeat at this point the caution made about generalizations concerning the various communities since I am now going to make a few generalizations, largely from historical and culture perspectives.

The modern communities of this diaspora are chiefly descended from participants in the forced trans-Atlantic migration of Black people from Africa during a period of approximately 300 years from 1550 to 1850. Of the 12 million or so people who constituted these arriving immigrants, a very large number were never biological parents, so voracious was the plantation system of human life. The actual African parentage of modern diasporic communities is a complex mosaic and must take account of both European and Amerindian input. These variables, African, Amerindian, European must be factored in with such historical data as climatic zones, dates of settlement, types of agricultural and arterial economy and modes of production before adequate typologies of diasporic communities can be devised.

Such typologies are a necessary step in the study and appreciation of the diaspora. To quote from a paper I wrote several years ago, the majority of African-descended people of the Western Hemisphere are to be regarded as culturally descended from an African culture complex which has been modified by European and Amerindian contact. They indeed constitute a group of related provinces of the African world, in spite of the diverse political regimes under which they lived.

It is important to note that these political regimes have rarely been responsive to this mass of black folks even in the few instances where they have been Black-controlled. Certain parallelisms, in the present condition of the modern African states themselves come to mind, but are not essential to our purpose. An examination of these Western Hemisphere provinces of African culture should find that most culture traits therein may be assigned a place on a theoretical scale of Africanity ranging from purely African forms to highly admixed forms.

A useful scale would designate the following nodes: **(a)** the purely African form; **(b)** Creolized forms; **(c)** embedded forms.

The *African forms* are those which faithly reflect forms present in the black African core or forms derived from these without admixture of other forms.

The *Creolized forms* are those forms based on a fusion of African and non-African analogs. The embedded forms are those with non-African analogs in which the African component causes a radical innovation, creating in the process a new form.

To give you quick examples from music, there does exist throughout, in various parts of the diaspora, but particularly in Haiti and in Brazil, purely African music which has survived in connection with religious ritual. There exists in many parts of the diaspora, musical forms which clearly result from a fusion, such as jazz in the United States, the samba in Brazil, the rumba in Cuba, the tango in Argentina, all of which I would call creolized form.

Embedded forms are forms which are to be found, in say, the music of a composer like Scott Joplin where the music clearly derives from some acquaintanceship with Chopin, but it has something in it that Chopin didn't know 'bout.

The significance of our understanding the Afro-centric

element in the composition and culture of the diaspora is great at this critical moment when many of the most positive features of African heritage are under assault and in disarray throughout the diaspora. My footnote to that is that we lament, to a considerable extent, the neglect of African culture. I submit to you that a great many people who you pass in the street, under the age of 30, are in no sense descendants of African culture. They are aliens. One has to reach out to get them in, but it is not getting them back in, they've never been in.

I will conclude by repeating that it is only in the last two decades that the term African Diaspora has been generally used. The usage bespeaks a heightening of consciousness which is important and salutary. Ways must be devised of utilizing that heightened consciousness, both in the extension of our knowledge and in the education of the young.

SECTION III

CURRICULUM METHODOLOGY AND STRATEGY

... the American educational system, as it is, is not designed for the benefit of Black people, who are oppressed by that system; it is not designed to facilitate the regeneration of a people it has calculatedly debased; it is not designed to liberate the spirit of the sons and daughters of Africa nor to enhance that spirit nor to thrill at its soaring; the American educational system is not designed to encourage the destruction of the American political and economic system, no matter how cruel and debilitating embattled minorities may find that system.

That the American educational system, as it is, is designed to benefit and to maintain the status and well-being of the white middle class majority; it is designed to train the personnel and to maintain the ideology which will ensure the perpetuation and endurance of the American political and economic system, which is now, and always has been, hostile to the ultimate aims of the Black minority which serves it.

—Hoyt W. Fuller

Ivan Van Sertima, Ph.D.
Professor of African Studies
Rutgers University

Dr. Van Sertima is a Professor of African Studies at Rutgers University and also Visiting Professor at Princeton University. He is the Editor of the Journal of African Civilizations. Recent books he has edited include: *Blacks in Science: Ancient and Modern, Black Women in Antiquity, Egypt Revisited, Nile Valley Civilizations, African Presence in Early Asia, African Presence in Early Europe, African Presence in Early America, Great African Thinkers* and *Great Black Leaders: Ancient and Modern.*

Ivan Van Sertima was born in Guyana, South America. He was educated at the School of Oriental and African Studies, London University and the Rutgers Graduate School and holds degrees in African Studies, Linguistics and Anthropology.

Future Directions for African and African-American Content in the School Curriculum
BY IVAN VAN SERTIMA

It is indeed a great pleasure and a great honor to be here today. One is very much aware of the enormous energy, the growing force with which we are moving ahead in changing our curriculum and bringing into it the breath, the new breath, the new wind that is blowing across the world.

I want to dedicate this lecture today to Dr. Cheikh Anta Diop, our good friend and brother, who died a year and a half ago, because his spirit is very much with us today.

We had his colleague, Dr. Theophile Obenga, from the Congo with us a few days ago in Washington, D.C. and his work has been translated into English for the first time. *Egypt Revisited* the new book out from *The Journal of African Civilizations* startles us, because one of the things that has been claimed is that since Africans were basically inferior and created no great civilization and had no science and because Egypt was open to Europe and open to Asia, it is quite possible that Europeans and Asians trickled into Egypt, creating the grand civilization and then carried the light of civilization down to their black barbaric brothers in the south.

What *Obenga* has shown—and I'll come to *Diop* in a moment, but what *Obenga* has shown which has not been shown before with such clarity and force is that the vision of God and of the universe among the Africans in Egypt is different from that among the Europeans and the Asiatics. In fact, we now know that they had an idea that is very close to modern physics. They saw the world in the beginning as a kind of **plasma,** something in an **aqueous state,** and there was this primal stuff or matter in which there was a certain vibration which then left a certain consciousness. This consciousness eventually evolved until there emerged what we call God, who then reconstituted the physical universe. We may never know how the world began, but in terms of its poetry, its consistency, its intuitive logic, its modernity, its complexity, and its sophistication, it has no equal anywhere until modern times.

If Europe or Asia had created Egyptian civilization, how come their vision of that God and that universe was so different? When we look at other aspects of culture, like the language of the Egyptians, Cheikh Anta Diop showed thousands of intimate inter-connections between African languages in inner-Africa and with Egyptian language.

We had thought, and Chancellor Williams and even I had said in our books, 'that is an Afro-Asiatic language.' Now we have proof beyond any question that the Egyptian language is not Afro-Hamitic or Afro-Asiatic or Afro-Semitic or Afro-anything. It is fundamentally African.

Those elements that came in later from other places and other peoples, those are surface elements, lexical elements, words here and there which come into every language. They have nothing to do with the fundamental grammatical structure of Egyptian language which is African.

Their writing is African. We had thought the hieroglyphics originated in Egypt. That is not so. In 1962, an American team, under Keith Seele, discovered a Pharaonic civilization south of Egypt, in Nubia, in Ethiopia. Many people have tried to put Ethiopia in the evening of Egyptian civilization. We know now it was the dawn. We have found 12 Black Pharaohs reigning in the Nile Valley at a place called Ta-Seti at least two centuries before the first Egyptian dynasty. Hence, the structure of Pharaonic civilization, the god Horus, the son of Osiris, the figure of Horus the son of Osiris. The Falcon god Horus. The Crown of the South. The hieroglyphics, the palace facades and palace serekhs are already found there in the south of Egypt before it moves up into Egypt. It's not found in Asia. It's not found in Europe. How could they found the civilization?

If it is they who were coming and founding the civilization, where are **their** plants? The whole plant life, all the cultivated plants in pre-Dynastic and early-Dynastic Egypt are African. The watermelon had come in. Cultivated cotton, Gossypium herbaceum had come in. Oil palm fruit had come in. The bottle gourd, lagenaria had come in. When we go down to these things we can establish that history you see, major history, is never truly lost.

History is only lost when we lose it. If we allow ourselves to forget, then it is truly lost. Nothing is lost that is contained in consciousness and even in the ground, when we have thought that we had forgotten it all, that it is truly lost, we find that the shattered world of Africa can be pieced together again. It has to be pieced together in our consciousness so that we, not only Africa, can be whole again. It is the beginning of a different kind of world, a different kind of African, and a different kind of humanity itself because this is not just for Africans. *The European has strayed for a long time and it is necessary that he be brought back into the fold of humanity as much as the brother he has enslaved.* That is why history is so vital and important to us.

You look at other things, their circumcision, their totemism, their forms of divine kingship, it is all African. So culturally, it is African. Physically it is clearly not homogeneous. Egypt is not homogeneous. Even in early times there are people trickling in from Europe and Asia. But in the times they are trickling in, they are nomads. They have no major civilization. They had no profound influence on that civilization until much later in the day when the Greeks and Romans came, by which time classical Egyptian civilization had ceased to be classical Egyptian civilization.

We have to be very clear about that. *You can go to Egypt now and unless you look most carefully and you go in certain places you will not find the truly indigenous native Egyptian.*

Just like in America, in this room there are very few native Americans. They are people who came in later, Europeans, Africans, etc. The native is elsewhere. He's in parts of South America. He is in Mexico. He is in other parts. He's in the forests of Guyana, etc. So that native American civilization is not modern American civilization.

When Cortez, the first European entered America, he was startled by the sophistication of the native American. When he went to Teotihauacan, which was then the center of America, long before the United States was a twinkle in anyone's eye, Cortez said, "When I saw their pyramids and their palaces and their temples and their floating gardens at Chiapas and the most advanced agriculture techniques then found in the world known only in medieval Mali, only medieval Ghana and Mexico, and their aqueducts and their reservoirs and their zoos and their running water," he said, "I have not seen its like anywhere."

Likewise in Egypt, when we were in Dallas about a year ago we managed to get the Egyptian Minister of Culture fired because in the middle of the big dispute we were having, he came out to say that Egypt is neither Black nor White and that Blacks have no real claim to Egyptian heritage. They call it "my culture." How could it be his culture? The late Arab invasion has nothing to do with classical Egyptian civilization just as the late European invasion of America has nothing to do with Native American civilization.

When Reagan was in Moscow and talking about how he dragged the Native American up, the Native American appeared in Moscow and said, "He has nothing to do with this." Poor Reagan, he would not know the difference anyway. Even with the new hole in his head, an operation that should have been performed long ago.

Let us look at the physical characteristics of the Egyptian. This can be very confusing for students and scholars because there are some Egyptians who are not African. You must remember there have been invasions of Egypt.

INVASIONS OF EGYPT (AFRICA)

Hyksos Invasion	1600 B.C.
Assyrian Invasion	650 B.C.
Persian Invasion	525–405/ 343–332 B.C.
Greek Invasion	332–30 B.C.
Roman Invasion	30–395 A.C.E.

Egypt was attacked by the Hyksos around 1660 B.C. For 150 years there is no pharaonic dynasty. Egypt was attacked by the Assyrians who at around 664 or 650 B.C. defeated the Africans and pushed them back into the south, and it took quite a while to push them out.

Then it was attacked by the Persians under Cambyses, that lunatic who had no respect for civilization, who decided to raze everything to the ground, and then it was attacked by the Greeks. There comes this beginning of the serious real story, because the first Europeans, the Greeks, were in awe of the Africans. They could not understand how anyone had gone that far. *Greece had its genius, but nothing compared to what the Egyptians had achieved.* The African had reached levels that startled the Greeks' levels in astronomy, in mathematics. His literature, his philosophy startled them. They were to feed on that as they came in even as I now, out of my shattered world have had to go to Europe to be educated, then did the great Europeans come to Africa to be educated. Thales, Democritus, Pythagoras, Euxodus, Anaximenes, Anaximander—all of these people came and sat at the foot of Africans and they said so. There was no question about it, as *Martin Bernal* points out in *Black Athena,* it was not until around the 1830s that Europeans, feeling guilt about their enslavement of the Africans, decided to try and prove that the African had nothing to do with civilization. They started to question even what the Greeks had said. The Greeks said clearly, that even old Zeus was African; they worshiped Black women as goddesses. Artimus, the goddess of chastity is a black woman in Greece. Circe in the *Odyssey* is represented not only as a Black woman but with African features. You can see the picture that Larry Williams brought to our attention in *Black Women in Antiquity*.

Andromeda, who married the Greek hero poet Perseus, is represented with European features but Black face because black was considered to be a symbol of beauty. Minerva, the goddess of Wisdom, is represented as a Black woman. Medea, who helped Jason win the golden fleece, is represented in Grecian vases as a Black woman. They were so fascinated by things Black. And the reason was because Black, then, was associated with excellence. Because when they looked around them they saw things that startled them.

The pyramids are not a joke. Let me tell you a story about that. The Japanese, who we regard today as the great technocrats of the world, the people who have superior technological mastery of things, the Japanese tried to build a pyramid. A little one, mind you.

In Egypt, in 1978, they started out by taking bronze tools. Diop had made it clear that it was impossible to cut granite the way they were cutting. The Africans were blasting through mountains. This is not only above the ground, they were going under the ground. You look at those things. That's not a joke. It's not easy to build. Diop showed that things found in the study of the pyramids that made it quite clear that you were dealing with advanced iron smelting. These are not bronze tools cutting through granite like laser beams. But the Japanese insisted, they took the tools they thought were the most advanced tools at that time. They tried to cut the stone. The tools broke. Do you know how they cut the stones? With 20th century technology using air jack hammers.

Then they thought that all you had to do now, you take these stones—and those stones that the Japanese cut were not as large as the African stones. The highest they went was about 10 tons. Most of them were two plus ton stones. The Africans were taking 50 ton stones and putting them on the top of their skyscrapers without being an inch off.

The Japanese tried to put that stone on the barges that they built which they thought were the Egyptian-type barges and the barges capsized.

Once again reversion to 20th century technology, steam boats. So then they brought it into the desert. Then they tried to pull it out of the boat, to bring it in to build a pyramid. It sank in the sand.

They made a big effort to drag it. Then when they tried to put it up they found that the Hollywood version of all these slaves, 'Heave ho, Heave ho,' *it wouldn't work.*

Then they used 20th Century cranes. When they used 20th Century cranes the stone got chipped, broken and scratched. When they went to the casing stone of the African pyramid, built 5,000 years ago, there is not a single stone that is broken or scratched.

They tried to put it in alignment. In the morning when they thought nobody could see them they brought out their helicopters. Do you know they could not put it in alignment? Do you know that the alignment the Africans achieved at the height of the Pyramid Age was 1/1000th of an inch of mathematical perfection? Only people who deal with cutting eyeglasses, only people who cut jewels today can achieve that perfection.

In other words, they were bringing the eye of the jeweler to the task of the stone mason. They were using the sorts of things we use for minute material on acres of stone.

Now where is that in Asia and Europe at that time? Or even after? Yet we have all these stories about the pyramid building race. If there was a pyramid building race, where are their pyramids?

Dr. Cheikh Anta Diop developed a method for studying melanin in the skin. He pointed out to them the Greeks and Romans who saw, they weren't speculating, they saw the people who they were dealing with. They had fought with them. They had worked with them. They had lived with them. They said they were "black-skinned and woolly haired."

Margaret Shinnie said that the reason they said they were

black was just subjective like the way Norwegians would call Italians black. So Diop pointed out that *Herodotus* went further than saying they were black—he said that 'they had woolly hair.'

We were in the museum, my wife and I, Dr. Hilliard took us to Egypt, and we went into the Cairo Museum to photograph wigs. Do you know those wigs do not have a number. Everything is catalogued in the Cairo Museum but you can't find the numbers on the wigs—they're scattered all over the place. And the one of them which has a number and is identified they call it "Lion's Mane."

In other words, we have to believe that a lioness was plaiting the hair of a lion in order to get African hair. And then when we can't see the skin anymore, fortunately we have excellent photographs of the skin. Dr. Hilliard showed me a photograph of Anut Tawi, an African princess who died about 4,000 years ago.

You can see her teeth. You can see the texture of her skin. You can see her hair, her African hair. I have seen people in the coffins, recently dead, not looking as good as that. They ran a rumor through Egypt that the reason we can't watch the mummies is because Sadat said it was not right, it was undignified. It was desecrating, etc. I'm sure Sadat never said anything of the sort. But you see you have once again an attempt to push that African aside.

Cheikh Anta Diop and myself, we made special efforts to get the Egyptians to reclaim the splinters of the Sphinx's chin and part of the nose. They were reluctant. Eventually they moved on the British and the British felt embarrassed. They did not know what to do and essentially they allowed the splinters to go back to Egypt on "permanent loan." Of course you know there is no such thing. But we have to be very afraid about how those modern Egyptians are going to put back that nose. It may be necessary, though I much regret it, that just as how the French blew it off in the first place we may have to blow it off in the second.

The Melanin Dosage Test that Cheikh Anta Diop developed which is accepted now in the United States, show that the depth of melanin between the *derm* and the *epiderm* of mummies in the Museum of Man show that those are Africoid types. He was not allowed to take square inches of skin from the mummies in the Cairo Museum.

The latest skeletal studies show that the skeletons, that the skull of Egyptians are the same in the pre-Dynastic period as they are in the Middle Kingdom which is about 1,000 years later. Yet all of these other things, William McIver, etc. and Falconberger have said that only 36 percent are Negro, another 35 percent are Intermediate Brown Mediterraneans and 11 percent are Cro-Magnon which is the white and the rest we don't know. The so-called 35 percent Diop showed, if you took those measurements and took it into Africa where there are pure races unmixed, you would find the same measurements as the Intermediate Brown Mediterranean types.

All of this was done because it was difficult for Europeans to admit that those people whom they had enslaved as Volney said, had one time given them a lot of their art and sciences.

You cannot imagine how profound is the contribution of Africa in early times to the European civilization. You cannot read a single philosophical treatise of the Greeks without being able, as Diop has shown in studying the philosophy of the Pharaonic Empire, of the Pharaonic period, without falling heavily upon the ideas, distorted though it later was, of the Egyptians.

As *Obenga* has shown, the Africans at that time were writing when he reads the translation. It reads like if you're reading *Jean Paul Sartre* or *Heidegger* or *Kierkegaard.* It is very complex. The level of philosophical discourse was sophisticated. We have found recently in the British Museum, *Obenga* tells us, evidence that they had actually worked out the speed of light. Do you know what that is? Light is actually seen as protons, separate discreet parts, as well as streams. We only learned about that in the 20th century. The Egyptians had already been working on that.

They were already telling us that light went many, many meters below the surface of the oceans. We didn't know that. That's *very* recent. Dr. Charles S. Finch shows us that when you study the Edwin Smith papyrus, which was merely recently retranslated or redone around 15 something B.C. but which had been done much earlier, that you find these people who had done diagnoses which we are unable to do today without x-rays, and that they had actually found the **locus** of the brain where auditory information is processed. All of that is 20th century stuff. We were already doing that.

But let me say this, that it has come, the time has come to use Dr. Leonard Jeffries, Jr. This great explosion of knowledge has become so dramatic that it is impossible to stop the tide.

Only our ignorance, only our weakness, only our inability to be precise, only our tendency to be simply propagandistic can destroy the thrust of that knowledge. We have to be extremely careful. Because, when you look at the obelisk I saw at Aswan last year, the fallen obelisk, the one they did not erect, because they said it had a flaw. And I searched for the flaw. It was hard to find the flaw. You wondered about the perfection of these people, the ideal of perfection and you understand why African men operated at that level. It's not enough to have brains. You have to use it in a special way. We can't just do any old thing, throw any old scholarship around. Now that we have the facts, we have to learn the great detail.

There are a people, I don't have to mention them, who learned a lot about the detail of their history and they are on the top of the world, even if you say boo, about that history they've got you. They made that history sacred and you can't quarrel with that. *When we make our history as sacred as religion it will make a difference.*

We have to be able to chant these things. Our children chant them like poems so that nobody who could come afterwards and tell them, "You know this began with the Greek Herophilus, who created pulse-taking," when in fact you could go back to early papyri of the Africans in Egypt and find pulse-taking 1,000 years before Herophilus. You're going to tell me that Hippocrates started the details of fractures of the clavicle and dislocation of the mandible when you can go back to the Edwin Smith Papyrus, long before the birth of Hippocrates, and find the same detail in the same language.

You're going to tell me that Europeans created geometry when geometry was a response to the complex inundations of the Nile. Nobody on earth was aware of the precise revolution of the earth around the sun to come up with the 365 and a quarter day year. The Sumerians are supposed to have helped Egyptian civilization. They did not have a 365 and a quarter day year. The Africans created the 365 and a quarter day year which we are using now. It's very precise. They created the most intelligent and accurate calendar. Even their enemies say so. They created the Leap Year. We no longer have a Leap Year. We call it the Leap Year, but that's a Leap Day. Every four years we have a Leap Day in February. They had a true Leap Year every 1,460 years. They jumped a year. Then they were left with the 365 and they cut off five days, five festival days; they created Christmas, December the 25th was worshiped and revered and celebrated by the Africans in Egypt as a Day of Horus which was their Christ figure. Christ is an African word, *Krst*. Egyptian. Africa is an African word. *Afruika* meaning beginnings.

You see it in their language, it isn't lost. Do not for one moment think, inspite of all the enslavement and in spite of all the destructions that have occurred, there is still the evidence. Kenti, where the civilization came from the South, Kenti means South. You know what it also means in Egyptian, first. They didn't forget it. It is in their language.

The signs are there. And it is not just in Egypt. Egypt gave us all of these things. You go into medicine. You are startled by the depths. They were actually performing operations that startle us. We find many of these things discussed, gynecology, ecology, pregnancy, diagnosis, treatment of abscesses and burns, studies of the pulse, studies in diagnostic precaution, etc. All that is there 2,600 years before the birth of Christ. And as Dr. Finch showed, that was merely being rewritten afterwards. It could have existed even before that time.

They were the first people to have specialists, specialists of the ear, specialists of the nose, specialists of the mouth, not just general physicians. They only have one chapter on magic.

If you were to move into inner Africa you do not find any difference. All anthropology focused heavily on tribal, I shouldn't misuse the word, but they focus on little people, peripheral people. That's why we have thousands of books about Africans and they have no science.

When I was going to university in London, I was told that "the Africans were pre-literate. They never read nor wrote." I did not know that the people who were telling me that were the pre- literates.

English has no writing system. We have English sounds, English words, we do not have a writing system in English. We use the Roman writing system. The French have no writing system. The English have no writing system. The Spanish have no writing system. The Germans have no writing system. They're all using the Roman System. Only a few tribes in Europe have developed writing systems. The Romans, the Greeks and there is the Syrellic Alphabet in Russia, and there is the Celtic which is half and half. *The Book of Balemore* tells us that 'half of the Celts are Africoid types.' The Phoenicians borrowed a lot from the Egyptians. Africa has just as many writing systems. Africa has hieroglyphics, which were to affect so many other writing systems.

Africa has the *meroitic* which we are trying to decipher at UNESCO. Africa has *Akan* script, both a drum script and a written script. Africa has the *Farka* script, the only script that travels from Africa to America during slave times. It is being used in the jungles of South America by the *Saramanka*, even to this day. Africa has the *Mande* script which has variance, modern variance like the via.

There are thousands of inscriptions in these things. No people has left their literature from the Old World as complex and as reserved as the African. There is no book in the world as old as *The Book of the Dead* which is really *The Book of the Coming Forth By Day.* It's African.

So we have nothing to be ashamed of. We have no reason to exaggerate and make up myths about ourselves because history is more startling than any myth.

Our history, if studied closely and recorded precisely is far more startling than anything that we could dream of. So it is not necessary to make it up or to inflate anything because all we have to do is to look at it very closely. You go into Inner Africa, into the centers which they did not study, they are finding steel smelting machines. They are finding techno-logical innovation by Africans far in advance of Europe. They found steel smelting machines in Tanzania that were used 1,500 to 2,000 years ago in an industrial site, mind you, in East Africa. There they found the population was more dense than it is today because it was properly supported. It wasn't broken down and shattered by colonization.

In that area they found Africans with their machines of which they found 13 under the ground. Africans producing steel in the middle of the Iron Age at temperatures of 1,850 degrees centigrade. The highest achieved in Europe was 1,620 degrees in the 2nd Century Roman blast furnace. They found the African was producing steel through iron crystallization and they were doing it in one single stage whereas Europe, even in the middle of the 19th Century took two crude pro-cesses to produce steel. And in order to produce these iron crystals they had to enter semi-conductor technology 1,500 years ago. Semi-conductor technology only came to Europe at the end of the 19th, early 20th Century. And on top of that they found Africans were using less fuel because they had less fuel at their disposal. And that brings us to the fact that most people do not realize.

The United States reports Africa has less jungle than any other continent comparable with its land space. By that has meant Africa has less jungle than South America. Africa has less jungle in terms of land space, comparable land space, than two Europes which would be the comparable land space of Africa. But we get all this fascination about 'the African is related to the jungle, he is a man of nature.' There are no men of nature. Man jumps out of nature. Man takes nature and shapes it. Man makes things. He has always, from the beginning, that is the beginning of science. We are not out of it. As I pointed out to Congress, most of the machines and instruments that were being used by Columbus and Vespucci were not of European origin. Even the gun, the chemistry of gunpowder being brought out of China by the Moors and it was made into the fire stick by the Muslims who attacked the Indians with it, then the Europeans took it and refined it and made it the greatest weapon of enslavement. The *caravele* (sic) which Columbus and Vespucci used comes from the *Caravorse* which is Arabic, which comes from the *Pangalos* which the Africans and Arabs are using on the Indian Ocean.

The compass on the ship is not European. And the astrilobe on the ship is not European. The sails of the ship were not European. They are Arab-Latin sails which Arabs and Africans were using on other oceans.

There is something far more serious which has been just pushed aside. The Moors. On the edge of the Industrial Revolution, when Europe had been in the Dark Age, came the Moors. Who were these Moors? They were a mixed bag. Yes, they were not all Black Africans, but of the 7,000 troops that attacked Europe, 6,000 were Black Africans. They included Berbers. There are both blue-eyed Berbers as well as Black Berbers. The smiths among the Berbers are all black. The metal workers. The people who were involved in metal smelting are the Black Berbers.

The Arabs too, came and intermarried. Early Arabia was all black but by the time of Mohammed it was only 10 percent black. But then those Arabians came, intermarrying and in the dynasties they established the Arabs and Africans, they established four dynasties in Europe. The Ommiyads, the Abasic, the Almoravids, the Amarrabe and the Almohades. And the Almoravids and the Almohades grew up under Senegal, those are mainly African dynasties.

The Moors surrendered in Grenada in 1492, the year Columbus sailed. If you see a picture drawn by the Spanish of the surrender of the Moors, who do you think is the general that is surrendering? Black faces. African features. How could they surrender if they didn't have power in Grenada? And people have tried to represent this in all sorts of ways. Do you know why? Because that chapter is the most critical chapter in early European history, prior to the Renaissance.

The Dark Ages had fallen on Europe, the glory of Greece and Rome had faded and by 711 A.D. when the Africans and Arabs attacked, Europe was far inferior in its sciences to the rest of the world because Greece and Rome had gone ahead. Their empires had put them far ahead of others. The Egyptians had gone into decline. But in that period Europeans slipped back again.

Then came the Moors. They introduced crank shafts. They introduced *worm* and *pinion* gears operated hydraulically. They introduced optics, the first eyeglasses in the world were made by the Moors. They introduced algebra. There was no algebra in Europe. They introduced gun powder. They introduced the gun and the fire stick. They introduced air conditioning for the first time in Europe, perfumed air conditioning. They took water from the mountains and ran it down in the lead pipes into the private houses. They introduced lighting. Not electric light, but light, they lighted the street. No street in Europe, London or Paris or elsewhere was lit before the Moors.

The Moors lit Cordova. You could walk for miles by the flash of lamps. They brought rice into Europe. They brought special strains of cotton into Europe. They brought strawberries and lemons and ginger into Europe. The finest fashions in the world were in Almeria where the Moors were. The finest silk and steel was in Damascus where the Moors were. The finest tanneries in the world were in Morocco where the

Moors were. The finest carpets were at Tudela where the Moors were. The finest mills and markets were in Cordova where the Moors were. We don't even know anything about it. We hear about this great Spanish victory and how they brought civilization to America. We'd better check that out very carefully.

Because there is no harm, you see, lots of people feel challenged by this. Europeans feel challenged. There is no need to feel challenged. That is the nature of civilization. You're supposed to borrow from each other. Cross-fertilization of cultures and people. That is what makes civilization. People who are not truly civilized are incestuous, isolated, primitive. Yet they are civilized sometimes more than the so-called civilized, because civilization is not just technology. It's the humanization of the human.

These things entered Europe. It inspired Europe. Europe had two universities. It was 99 percent illiterate when the Moors attacked, and so was the rest of the world. Only small cliques in the world read and wrote. secret societies in Africa and the trader groups in Africa. The same little cliques in Europe, in Asia, in America, but Europe had only two universities. The Arabs and Africans introduced seventeen universities into Europe. Everything that could be translated from the ancient and medieval work was brought into Europe by the Moors. Out of Egypt, out of the Arab world, out of Timbuktu and Sankore and other parts of Africa, out of Morocco, out of ancient Greece and Rome, everything that could be translated was brought into those universities.

It is true that an invasion, whatever way, wherever it comes from, does have its negative effects. But unlike the slavery that was to follow the Anglo-American slavery, the Western European type slavery, the Moors did not destroy the culture of the Spanish. They did not take away their language. They did not take away their legal systems. They did not take away their humanity. It is true that they insisted that they should have something, the election of Bishops, because the church then was as powerful as the state sometimes, even more powerful. And there are dark periods after Abdul Rahman or even under the reign of Abdul Rahman perhaps unknown to him, certainly not supported by him. There was a certain amount of white slavery by the Arabs and some of their brothers. But the science of that time, which was to leave such an impact on later times came out of that world. Came out of that Muslim world. So that it wasn't just in Egypt.

Let us not forget inner Africa. Inner Africa was to give us so much in the field of medicine, just let me point to one thing. Tetracycline, which we only began to use in the 1950s, they found tetracycline being used by Africans in Nubia fourteen centuries ago. We found the yellow/green ashes of tetracycline in the bones of Nubians and where we found it, we found the lowest incidence of infectious disease in an ancient population.

We found Africans were using the vaccine before us. Cotton Mather said that his slave, Onesimus, had brought a smallpox vaccine from Africa. The Africans gave us Orbaine. They gave us Capsicum. The gave us Kaopectate which we are now using for diarrhea. They gave us Resur Pine, the first drug that treats hypertension and psychotic disorder. They gave us Phisostigmania used for eye diseases. We don't know anything about that. All we know is we get these pictures of Africa.

When have you ever seen an African Parliament in session on television? When do you see even in Ali Mazuri's "Africans," how many dignified, powerful Africans do you meet in that series? Ali Mazuri, and let me give him his due because some parts of his series are quite good, but he is so ignorant of African technology. He goes to the edge of the river and he says, "Africans did not want to go out. They were content to fish in the rivers," nice little blacks. That comes over you know. They are not like the vicious expansionist Europeans. So they just fished in the rivers. What does he know about the boats of Africa? Africa has two of the longest rivers in the world, the Nile and the Niger. They have spent more time on those waters than they have spent on all the roads. They had about 12 types of ships on the Niger, not even counting the Nile which are 3,000 years of ship building. It gave its ideas to the Phoenicians, who were the great navigators of the early world.

You find, for example, on the Indian Ocean the moguls of India were so impressed by African ideas about the sea and their ships that they made them admirals of the Indian Ocean, a people known as the Siddis and African sea-going people were made admirals of the Indian Ocean by the moguls of India.

The Chinese report Africans were bringing elephants to them in ships to the Court of China two centuries before Columbus. You can't take elephants across the Indian Ocean in a dugout.

The catamaran in the Pacific . . . they found these jointed canoes which were not really canoes. Canoe was a misnomer. Jointed boats that were extremely sturdy, faster and sturdier than the Asiatic boats. They found one of them with 48 men, 24 rowing, 24 resting which could cross so fast, it could move from Puerto Rico to Venezuela in a single day. These are African boats. He knows nothing about that. The papyrus reed boat which Thor Heyerdahl built, or rather directed the building of because he financed it, he got the papyrus reed, 12,000 lbs. of papyrus reed, and Abdullah Djibrine, and the Buduma people reconstructed the papyrus reed boat and it crossed from Safi in North Africa all the way to Barbados in 1969. Showing that boats could have crossed from Africa to America more than 1,000 years before Christ because that boat was used as early as that. It is still in use.

Do you know they never steered to America. The currents took them from Africa to America. They went into the labs in America and they were startled when botanists discovered that two of the cottons in America, the only two major cultivated cottons in America, Gossypium Hirsutum and Gossypium Barbadense. When they were examined in the lab they found that of 26 chromosomes, 13 were African and 13 were American. And they couldn't understand how could an African cotton marry with American cotton 2,000 years before Columbus? Because that is roughly when the strain occurred.

You know what they said, "perhaps it floated from Africa by itself." No people ever migrated as much as Africans. When Eric the Red ran into Iceland he found black people. He reported it, "The Vikings found blacks among them. Thorhall the Hunter, Thorstein the Black, Africans among the Vikings."

When the Romans attacked Britain they found Africans. They said they were people as dark as the Ethiopians among the fair- skinned Britains. They found Africans in China. The first Emperor of China was a black man. The Japanese talk about their special warriors. They said, "In order to be brave you must have a bit of black in you." If they didn't have blacks among them, how do they come to these curious ideas? The black had to migrate out of Africa to go into Europe. It is only about 55,000 years ago that the major mutation occurred of the African in Europe. Everyone agrees now that Europe was only peopled by Africans. There were no Europeans. Europeans began when the Africans were caught in the Ice. Some people put it near Spain. Some people put it near southwestern Russia. There it became absolutely necessary to drop pigmentation. Because pigmentation is critical in order to shield you against ultra-violet radiation in the ice. I'm not talking about temperate zones like this. This is a joke. I'm talking about real ice. I am talking about Europe where they had miles of Europe, where they had ice a half mile thick. So I'm talking about that kind of ice. These people had to live in caves. They had to cover themselves with fur against the cold. And then on top of that, apart from those shields against the sun, there was the sun coming through filters, because we never really see the sun here. It was a very unusual day here when you really see the sun. If you really want to know what the sun looks like, go live where I live, on the Equator. Between twelve and two, if you looked up at the sun you would be blinded. It's impossible to look at the sun between twelve and two. It's a burning ball of white fire in the sky.

Not here, because we have filters. So could you imagine that situation where in order to mineralize the bones you have to have Vitamin D and the pigmentation interferes with it. So only some of the Eskimos remain black because they had fish oil that could give men Vitamin D. But those people who could not assimilate that had to drop so that the melanocytes became such that they would have to drop. The melanocytes became largely inactive, producing a type which still have Africoid features. The broad nose, the expansive features of the tropics, but then the pink skin. Then later on you have the tendency for longer hair to protect the neck from cold as against close cropped hair which allows heat to dissipate. Then you have the narrow nose which is more effective in warming cold air. And you have contraction of this against the expansion of this and that.

These are very, very simple things basically. They have nothing to do with superiorities and inferiorities. They are man's response to different ecological environments just as the Asiatic had to develop a epicantic fold.

The Japanese and the Chinese have their epicantic fold, because they could not protect the eye in the winds as they trekked across the Asiatic Steppes. To protect the eye they had to develop a fold, which Europeans and Africans do not have.

So there is no big mystery anymore about race. There are lots of fights going on but three universities have come out; Hawaii, Berkeley, Oxford of all places, and they have made it quite clear that the founding population of the modern world is African.

We're not talking about man began in Africa. Apes began in Africa, too. That's no big deal. We're talking about the discoveries that man, not only the first man began in Africa, but the last man. That is about 250,000 years ago. Scientists have traced all the men and women now living on the earth to a black woman in Africa about 250,000 years ago. They could do it with great precision by checking out things in the blood. They know at what point this genetic mutation occurred. So man is far more united as a family than most of us have believed. And as I say, there is no point in the European feeling, 'Oh we are challenging his conception of his self image.' He has destroyed the self-image of our people for centuries. We have come to reclaim history because we want to show that the equality of man is not rooted in any biblical fantasy or liberal cliche. It is rooted in hard historical reality.

Until we understand that we cannot escape the sense of littleness. We have to use the first for our future as we enter the 21st Century. We have to use before us the standards of excellence that inspired our ancestors in Egypt and other places.

We have to stop being satisfied at mediocrity. Black stood for excellence. Black was the color for divinity among the Pharaohs. Red was used on men, red ochre was used on men and they thought they were red people. They weren't red people. Red ochre was used for thousands of years for Africans to signify vitality because it's the color of blood.

Yellow was used as fertility for women. So when you see red-faced men and yellow-faced women, look closely at the features, not the coloration, because those are conventions.

Black was for divinity, so in order to be a god you have to be made black. They wold not have done that unless they were doing that in their own image. While it is true that Christ Jesus was a mix of all peoples because we have seen the first image of Jesus. Some people don't believe he existed. But the first image, physical image of him is on a coin of Justinian II where you see a European Emperor and on the other side you see a man with dark brown skin and wooly hair like in Revelations and a Semitic nose indicating the mixing of people. And it was no crime for Europe to represent later, on the Michelangelo, who drew his family for Jesus. It was no crime for them to represent Jesus as white because people have a right to represent god or a prophet in their own image.

The Greeks represented Buddha as a Greek even though they knew his root.

It becomes a crime because we have been made to believe it is the literal truth.

We have been made to believe for centuries that the only people who invented things, created things, were the Europeans. That's why we come back now aggressively and as one great army, to reclaim that history. Because we have got to be whole again. Shattered though my word may be it can be pulled together because nothing is finally lost in consciousness. Bell Lab reported about 10 years ago the sound of the universe when it exploded. It is still around us. Nothing has left us.

Last year we photographed a star that died 165,000 years ago. We actually photographed the time it died. Because light events and sound events are never truly lost in the universe.

When I wrote *They Came Before Columbus*, I and only a few people suggested that in the Sahara, the evidence suggests from the spread of linguistic networks, from the spread of scripts, from the movement of bodies and plants, etc. that there were river valleys in the Sahara that linked it to the Nile Valley.

Three and a half years ago one of our space satellites sent down microwave beams into Africa, sixteen feet below the African earth and they found the river valleys just where one had suggested it would be. That Saharan-Sudanic Complex links us to the Nile Valley. So let me close by a poem to my brother Cheikh Anta Diop:

Too Soon
Too Soon
The banner draped for you
I would prefer a banner in the wind
Not bound so tightly with the scarlet fold
Not sudden sudden with your people's tears
But borne aloft
Down and beyond this dark dark lane of hate

Dear Comrade

If it must be that I no longer speak with you
No longer walk with you
No longer march with you
Then I must think of patience and of calm
For even now a greener leaf explodes
Sun-brightened stone
And all the rivers burn
Now, from the morning vanguard moving on
Dear Comrade
I salute you and I say

Death will not find us thinking that we die.

A Reading Guide for the Study and Teaching of African World History
BY JOHN HENRIK CLARKE

This reading guide is designed as an introduction to African World History which will stimulate a continuous study of the subject. In the 30 sessions outlined here, African history and its relationship to world history will be explained. The reading guide will start with an examination of the evidence that tends to prove that mankind originated in Africa. Special attention will be paid to all the main currents of African history such as: Africa at the Dawn of History and the Beginning of Organized Societies, the Early Empires of the Western Sudan, West Africa and the Grandeur of African Civilizations before the coming of the Europeans, the Decline of the Great Nation States of Africa and the Development of the Slave Trade, Colonialism and African Resistance. Additional sessions will be outlined as a teacher-student seminar. Such subjects as "The Role of the Arabs in Africa," "The Role of Women in Early Independent African Nations," and a detailed study of "How and Why the Slave Trade Came" will be included.

RATIONALE

African History is part of world history. It is a very old part and it is a very important part. There is no way to understand world history without an understanding of African history. A distinguished African-American poet, Countee Cullen, began his poem "Heritage" with the question: "What is Africa to me?" In order to understand Africa, we must extend the question by asking, "What is Africa to Africans?" and "What is tion by asking, "What is Africa to Africans?" and "What is Africa to the world?" With these questions we will be calling attention to the need for a total reexamination of African history. Considering the old approaches to African history and the distortion and confusion that resulted from these approaches, a new approach to African history must begin with a new frame of reference. What exactly are we talking about? We must be bold enough to reject such terms as "Black Africa" which presupposes that there is a legitimate "White Africa." We must reject the term "Negro Africa" and the word "Negro" and all that it implies. This word, like the concept of race and racism grew out of the European slave trade and the colonial system that followed. It is not an African word and it has no legitimate application to African people. For more details on this matter, I recommend that you read the book, *The Word Negro—Its Origin and Evil Use*, by Richard B. Moore, American Publishers, New York. In a speech on "The Significance of African History," The Caribbean-American writer, Richard B. Moore has observed:

> The significance of African history is shown, though not overtly, in the very effort to deny anything worthy of the name of history to Africa and the African peoples. This widespread, and well nigh successful endeavor, maintained through some five centuries, to erase African history from the general record, is a fact which of itself should be quite conclusive to thinking and open minds. For it is logical and apparent that no such undertaking would ever have been carried on, and at such length, in order to obscure and bury what is actually of little or no significance.

> The prime significance of African history becomes still more manifest when it is realized that this deliberate denial of African history arose out of the European expansion and invasion of Africa which began in the middle of the fifteenth century. The compulsion was thereby felt to attempt to justify such colonialist conquest, domination, enslavement, and plunder. Hence, this brash denial of history and culture to Africa, and indeed even to human qualities and capacity for 'civilization' to the indigenous peoples of Africa.

Mr. Moore is saying, in essence, that African history must be looked at anew and seen in its relationship to world history. First, the distortions must be admitted. The hard fact is that most of what we now call world history is only the history of the first and second rise of Europe. The Europeans are not yet willing to acknowledge that the world did not wait in darkness for them to bring the light, and that the history of Africa was already old when Europe was born. Until quite recently, it was rather generally assumed, even among well-educated persons in the West, that the continent of Africa was a great expanse of land, mostly jungle, inhabited by savages and fierce beasts. It was not thought of as an area where great civilizations could have existed or where the great kinds of these civilizations could have ruled in might and wisdom over vast empires. It is true that there were some notions current about the cultural achievements of Egypt, but Egypt was conceived of as European land rather than as a country of Africa. Even if a look at an atlas or globe showed Egypt to be in Africa, the popular thought immediately saw in the Sahara a formidable barrier and a convenient division of Africa into two parts: one (north of the Sahara) was inhabited by European-like people of high culture and noble history; the other (south of the Sahara) was inhabited by dark-skinned people who had no culture, and were incapable of having done anything in their dark and distant past that could be dignified by the designation of 'history.' Such ideas, of course, are far from the truth, as we shall see. But it is not difficult to understand why they persisted, and unfortunately still persist, in one form or another in the popular mind.

OBJECTIVE

The objective of this reading guide is to examine African history and its relationship to world history before and after the slave trade and the colonial period.

TEACHING METHODOLOGY

In most cases, the instructor should develop the subject of the sessions and place the information that relates to it in proper perspective so that a meaningful discussion can follow among the students and with the instructor. In these discussions, the subject should be viewed from many sides, and a comparison should be made between what the instructor has said and what was written in the required and general references relating to the subject. In these sessions the students will be expected to participate in the discussions following the formal lecture. If there are contradictions between what is said in the required readings and what is said by the instructor, these contradictions should be the basis for a class discussion.

RELEVANCE FOR THE STUDENT

This bold new look at the origin and development of African history and African people is both historical and topical. These sessions will answer some current questions, because the historical background to these questions will be looked at in a more honest and creative way. In the process of this approach to the history of African people, it is hoped that the student will take another look at world history and see how Africans relate to it.

The teacher of this subject should maintain that all history is a current event, because every event in history, in some way, still affects all mankind. In these sessions, both the instructor and the students should examine the great personalities, movements and events in history and their relevance for today.

AFRICA: ITS PLACE IN WORLD HISTORY FROM THE ORIGIN OF MAN TO 1600 A.D.
SECTION ONE

First Session:

   1. Why African History?

2. Why the Conflict Over African History?
3. The Relationship of African History to World History.

Main References

Africans and Their History, by Joseph B. Harris, pp. 1-25.
African History Outlined, by Carter G. Woodson, pp. 3-19.
African History, by Phillip D. Curtin, pp. 1-12.

Suggested References:

Introduction to African Civilization, by John G. Jackson, read
   Introduction to the book by John H. Clarke, pp. 3-35.
African History, by Basil Davidson, pp. 1-20.

For More Extensive Study

African Origins of Civilization: Myth or Reality, by Cheikh
   Anta Diop.
Civilization or Barbarism, by Cheikh Anta Diop.
Black Man of the Nile, by Yosef ben-Jochannan.
Africa: Mother of Western Civilization, by Yosef ben-
   Jochannan.
The African Origins of Major Western Religions, by Yosef ben-
   Jochannan.
Christianity Before Christ, by John G. Jackson.
Man, God and Civilization, by John G. Jackson.

Second Session:

1. Africa and the Origin of Man.
2. The Survival Achievements of Early Man in Africa.
3. Early Migrations of Men and Societies Within Africa.

Main References

Introduction to African Civilizations, by John G. Jackson, pp.
37-59.
Africans and Their History, by Joseph E. Harris, pp. 26-33.

African Saga: A Brief Introduction to African History. by Stanlake Samkange, pp. 11–34.

Suggested References

The Progress and The Evolution of Man in Africa, by L. S. B. Leakey, pp. 1–26.
The Prehistory of Africa, by J. Desmond Clark, pp. 46–64.
African and the Africans, by Paul Bohannon & Phillip D. Curtin, pp. 3–35.

For More Extensive Study

The following special issues of the *Journal of African Civilization,* edited by Ivan Van Sertima:

Africans in Early Asia
Africans in Early Europe

Third Session:

1. The Beginning of Organized Societies in Africa.
2. The Early African Begins to Master His Environment.
3. Early Migrations Outside of Africa.

Main References

African Saga, by Stanlake Samkange, pp. 35–36.
The Negro, W. E. B. DuBois, pp. 5–16
Introduction of African Civilizations, by John G. Jackson, pp. 37–59.

Suggested References

A Guide to African History, by Basil Davidson, pp. 1–10.
The History of Africa From the Earliest Times to 1800, by Harry A. Gailey, pp. 1–41.
Civilizations of Africa: Historic Kingdoms, Empires and Cultures, by George R. Pollack, pp. 3–11.

African Contribution (Part I), by John W. Weatherwax.

For More Extensive Study

The Destruction of Black Civilization, by Chancellor Williams
A History of Precolonial Black Africa, by Cheikh Anta Diop.
African Origins of Civilization: Myth or Reality, by Cheikh Anta Diop

Fourth Session:

1. The Southern Origins of Egyptian Civilization.
2. Western Scholarship and the Attempt to Take Egypt Out of Africa
3. The Africanness of Egypt.

Main References

Introduction to African Civilizations, by John G. Jackson, pp. 60–92
African Glory, by J. C. deGraft-Johnson, pp. 8–14.
Africans and Their History, by Joseph E. Harris, pp. 34–37.
African Saga, by Stanlake Samkange, p. 47.
Destruction of African Civilizations, by Chancellor Williams, pp. 62–100.
The Peopling of Ancient Egypt and the Deciphering of Meroitic Script, UNESCO's The General History of Africa Studies, Document 1.
General History of Africa, Document 11, see article, *The Origins of the Ancient Egyptians*, by Cheikh Anta Diop.

Suggested References:

The Progress of Evolution of Man in Africa, by L. S. B. Leakey, pp. 27–50.
History of Africa from Earliest Times to 1800, by H. A. Gailey, pp. 1–41.

History of African Civilizations, by E. Jefferson Murphy, pp. 18–36

For More Extensive Study

The following books by Gerald Massey:

Ancient Egypt the Light of the World, Vols. I & II.
The Natural Genesis, Vols. I & II.
Gerald Massey's Lectures
A Book of the Beginnings, vols. I & II.
African History Notebook, by William Leo Hansberry.

Fifth Session:

1. Egypt and the Golden Age.
2. New Revelations About the Life and Genius of Imhotep.
3. The Impact of Egypt on The Middle East and The Mediterranean World of Early Europe.

Main References

Introduction to African Civilizations, by John G. Jackson, pp. 93–152.
The Negro, by W. E. B. DuBois, pp. 5–10.
World's Great Men of Color, by J. A. Rogers, Vol. 1, pp. 38.
The Destruction of Black Civilizations, by Chancellor Williams, pp. 1–35.

Suggested References

Africa in History, by Basil Davidson, Chapter 2, pp. 11–41.
Africa, Its Empires, Nations and People, by Mary Penick Motley, pp. 1–46.
A History of the African People, by Robert W. July, 28–49.
A History of Egypt, by J. H. Breasted, pp. 69–95.

For More Extensive Study

A *History of the Modern World*, by R. R. Palmer & Joel Colton.
The Story of Africa, by Basil Davidson.
Shadow of the Third Century, by Alvin Boyd Kuhn.
Who is This King of Glory?, by Alvin Boyd Kuhn.
The Mediterranean World Ancient Times, by Eva Sanford.

Sixth Session:

1. Egypt: The Golden Age.
2. The Pharaohs of Fire, Flowers and Thunder.
3. Akhenaton viewed in the light of the earlier and the later development of Egypt. Did we stand at the threshold of a new age of man?

Main References

The World of Africa, by W. E. B. DuBois, pp. 98–114.
World's Great Men of Color, by J. A. Rogers, pp. 38–66.
African Saga, by Stanlake Samkange, pp. 55–72.

Suggested References

A History of Egypt, by J. H. Breasted, pp. 220–319.
A History of the African People, by Robert W. July, pp. 28–49
Great Civilizations of Ancient Africa, by Lester Brooks, pp. 28–82.

For More Extensive Study

The Ancient Egyptians and the Origin of Civilization, by G. Elliot Smith, Harper & Brothers, London/N.Y., 1923.
Akhenaton The Rebel Pharaoh, by Robert Silverberg, Chilton Books, Philadelphia/N.Y., 1964.
Ramesses II the Great Pharaoh and His Times, an exhibition in the City of Denver, by Rita E. Freed, 1987.
Africa in Antiquity, Vol. 1 & 11, The Brooklyn Museum, 1978.

Seventh Session:

1. The Rise of Cush.
2. The Cushite Conquest of Egypt.
3. A Review of Cushite Rule Over Egypt.

Main References

Introduction to African Civilizations, by John G. Jackson, Chapter 3, pp. 93–125.
The Destruction of Black Civilizations, by Chancellor Williams, pp. 41–57.
Suggested References

Lost Cities of Africa, by Basil Davidson, Chapter 3, pp. 23–47.
Civilizations of Africa, by G. F. Pollack, pp. 13–17.
Great Civilizations of Ancient Africa, by Lester Brooks, pp. 79–109.

For More Extensive Study

Nubia: Corridor to Africa, by Adam Smith, Princeton University Press.
The Lost Pharaohs of Nubia, by Bruce Williams.
Africa, The Wonder and the Glory, by Anna Melissa Graves.
Benevenuto Cellini Has No Prejudice Against Bronze, edited by Anna Melissa Graves, Waverly Press, Baltimore, 1942.

Eighth Session:

1. Ethiopia, North Africa and the Middle East.
2. Ethiopia and the Queen of Sheba.

Main References

Introduction to African Civilizations, by John G. Jackson, Chapter 2, pp. 60–92.
The Destruction of Black Civilizations, by Chancellor Williams, pp. 59–69.

Suggested References

A *History of the African People,* by Robert W. July, Chapter 2, pp. 28–49.
Great Civilizations of Ancient Africa, by Lester Brooks, pp. 33–40 and 230–231.
Civilizations of Africa, by G. F. Pollack, pp. 11–18.
Africa in History, by Basil Davidson, pp. 11–44.

For More Extensive Study

The Wonderful Ethiopians of the Ancient Cushite Empire, by Drusilla Dunjee Houston.
Ethiopia and the Origin of Civilization, by John G. Jackson.
The Africans: A Triple Heritage, by Ali A. Mazuri.

Ninth Session:

1. Egypt and Cush: End of the Golden Age.
2. The first European invasion of Africa.

Main References

African Glory, by J. C. deGraft-Johnson, pp. 8–24.
World's Great Men of Color, by J. A. Rogers, pp. 94–97.
The Destruction of Black Civilizations, by Chancellor Williams, pp. 71–90.

Suggested References

A *New History for Schools and Colleges,* by F. K. Buah, Book 1, pp. 101–210.

For More Extensive Study

North African Prelude, by Galbraith Welch.

Tenth Session:

1. Invaders of North Africa, general view: the Phoenicians, Greeks, Romans.
2. Africa and the Punic Wars.

Main References

African Glory, by J. C. DeGraft Johnson, pp. 25–36.
World's Great Men of Color, by J. A. Rogers, pp. 94–117.

Suggested References

Africa: Its Empires, Nations and People, by Mark Penick Motley, pp. 41–51.
A New History for Schools and Colleges, by F. K. Buah, Book 1, pp. 101–129.

For More Extensive Study

North African Prelude, by Galbraith Welch.

Eleventh Session:

1. The impact of invaders on North Africa: A general overview.
2. The Romans in Egypt.

Main References

African Glory, by J. C. deGraft-Johnson, pp. 15–24.
World's Great Men of Color, by J. A. Rogers, pp. 121–131.

Suggested References

The Lost Cities of Africa, by Basil Davidson, pp. 59–63.
A New History for Schools and Colleges, by F. K. Buah, pp. 87–88 and 134–140.
Africa: Its Empires, Nations and People, by M. P. Motley, pp. 53–69.

For More Extensive Study

North African Prelude, by Anna Melissa Graves.
The Mediterranean World in Ancient Times, by Eva Sanford.
Africa and the Modern World, by R. R. Palmer and Joel Colton,
    see Chapter on "The Rise of Europe."

Twelfth Session:

1. Africa and the Rise of Christianity: Part 1.
2. The African Woman in Early Christianity.
3. The Negative Impact of the Romans on Christianity.

Main References

African Glory, by J. C. deGraft-Johnson, Chapter 3, African
    Romans, pp. 25–52, Chapter 4, The North African Church.
Man, God and Civilization, by John G. Jackson.

Suggested References

African Glory, by J. C. deGraft-Johnson, pp. 37–52.
African Saga, by Stanlake Samkange, pp. 50–54.
Africa in History, by Basil Davidson, pp. 41–69.
Africa, Its Empires, Nations and People, by M. P. Motley, pp.
    53–68.

For More Extensive Study

North African Prelude, by Galbraith Welch.
Africa and Africans as Seen by the Classical Writers, by William
    Leo Hansberry.
Empires in the Desert, by Robert Silverberg.
History by Herodotus, trans. by George Rawlinson.

Thirteenth Session:

1. Africa and the rise of Christianity, Part II.
2. Christianity Again in Retrospect.

Main References

African Glory, by J. C. deGraft-Johnson, pp. 37–52.

Suggested References

African Origins of the Major Western Religions, by Dr. Yosef
    ben-Jochannan.
Sex and Race, by J. A. Rogers, Vol. 1, pp. 91–95.

For More Extensive STudy

Christianity Before Christ, by John G. Jackson.
Who is this King of Glory?, by Alvin Boyd Kuhn.
Shadow of the Third Century, by Alvin Boyd Kuhn.
Africa Mother of the Major Western Religions, by Dr. Yosef
    ben-Jochannan.

Fourteenth Session:

1. Africa and the Rise of Islam: Part 1.
2. Roman Misrule and the Corruption of Christianity
   as the Basis for the Rise of Islam.
3. The African Personality in the Making of Islam.

Main References

African Glory, by J. C. deGraft-Johnson, pp. 37–57.

Suggested References

The Horizon History of Africa, edited by Alvin M. Josephy, Jr.,
    Chapter IV, "The Spread of Islam," by John R. Willis, pp.
    137–149.
The Dawn of African History, edited by Roland Oliver, pp.
    30–26.
A New History for Schools and Colleges, by F. K. Buah, pp.
    141–172.

For More Extensive Study

Story of the Moors in Spain, by Stanley Lane-Poole.
Slavery and Muslim Society in Africa, by Allan G. B. Fisher &
   Humphrey J. Fisher.
Islam in Africa, by James Kritzeck and William H. Lewis.
Moorish Spain, by Enrique Sordo.

Fifteenth Session:

    1. Africa and the Rise of Islam: Part II.
    2. The Conquest of North Africa and Spain.

Main References

African Glory, by J. C. deGraft-Johnson, pp. 53–76.
Introduction to African Civilizations, by John G. Jackson,
   Chapter IV, pp. 157–193.

Suggested References

A New History for Schools and Colleges, by F. K. Buah, pp.
   148–155.
World's Great Men of Color, by J. A. Rogers, pp. 138–171.
Man, God and Civilization, by John G. Jackson, pp. 263–283.

For More Extensive Study

North African Prelude, by Galbraith Welch.
The Mediterranean World in Ancient Times, by Eva Sanford.
New General History of Africa, Vol. 1, UNESCO.

Sixteenth Session:

    1. The Rise of Ancient Ghana.
    2. The Formation of Ancient Ghana.

Main References

Topics in West African History, by Adu Boahen, pp. 3–8.
African Glory, by J. C. deGraft-Johnson, pp. 77–91.
African Heroes and Heroines, by Carter G. Woodson, pp. 25–31.
Introduction to African Civilizations, by John G. Jackson, pp. 196–219.

Suggested References

History of West Africa to the Nineteenth Century, by Basil Davidson, *pp.* 27–49.
Horizon History of Africa, edited by Alvin M. Josephy, J., Chapter V, "Kingdoms of the West Africa," pp. 177–185.

For More Extensive Study

A History of West Africa, by Jacob Ajayi and Michael Crowder.
Topics in West African History, New edition by Adu Boahen with Jacob Ajayi and Michael Tidy.
How Europe Underdeveloped Africa, by Walter Rodney.
History of West Africa, Vol. I & II, edited by J. F. Ajayi and Michael Crowder.

Seventeenth Session:

1. Sundiata, Spiritual Father of Mali.
2. The Rise of Mali.
3. Mali and the Reign of Mansa Mussa.

Main References

Topics in West African History, by Adu Boahen, pp. 13–17.
African Glory, by J. C. deGraft-Johnson, pp. 92–99.
African Heroes and Heroines, by Carter G. Woodson, pp. 25–36.
African Saga, by Stanlake Samkange, pp. 122–135.

Suggested References

History of West Africa, by Basil Davidson, pp. 52–60.
Ancient African Kingdoms, by Margaret Shinnie, pp. 56–73.
The Dawn of African History, edited by Roland Oliver, pp. 37–43.
"Africa's Golden Past," by William Leo Hansberry, Part IV, *Ebony Magazine, March 1965.*

For More Extensive Study

A Tropical Dependency, by Flora Shaw Lugard.
Travels and Discoveries in North and in Central Africa, by Heinrich Barth.
A History of Precolonial Black Africa, by Cheikh Anta Diop.

Eighteenth Session:

1. The Emergency of Sunni Ali.
2. The Rise of Songhay.
3. Prefaces to Greatness.

Main References

Topics in West African History, by Adu Boahen, pp. 23–32.
African Heroes and Heroines, by Carter G. Woodson, pp. 37–47
World's Great Men of Color, Vol. 1, by J. A. Rogers, p. 235.

Suggested References

A History of the African People, by Robert W. July, pp.65–70.
African History, by Basil Davidson, pp. 83–90.
African Saga, by Stanlake Samkange, pp. 136–147.
Ancient African Kingdoms, by Margaret Shinnie, pp. 73–86.

For More Extensive Study

Great Rulers of the African Past, by L. Dobler & W. A. Brown.
A Tropical Dependency, by Flora Shaw Lugard.
The Horizon History of Africa, edited by Alvin M. Joseph, Jr.

General History of Africa, Vol IV., UNESCO.

Nineteenth Session:

1. Trade and Commerce During the Administration of Muhammed Abubakr El-Touri.
2. The Career of Muhammed Abubakr El-Touri, Known as Askia the Great.
3. The Administration of the Songhay Empire by El-Touri.

Main References

Topics in West African History, by Adu Boahen, pp. 23–37.
African Glory, by J. C. deGraft-Johnson, pp. 100–109.

Special References

Great Rulers of the African Past, by L. Dobler & W. A. Brown, pp. 120–124.
Discovering Our African Heritage, by Basil Davidson, pp. 98–104.
A History of West AFrica, by Basil Davidson, pp. 65–72.

For More Extensive Study

History of West Africa, by Jacob Ajayi.
A Tropical Dependency, by Flora Shaw Lugard.
Lost Cities of Africa, by Basil Davidson.

Twentieth Session:

1. The Last Years of the Reign of Sunni Ali.
2. The Songhay Empire: The Death of Askia the Great.
3. Songhay: Beginning of the Troubled Years.

Main References

Topics in West Africa History, by Adu Boahen, pp. 32–37.

African Background Outlined, by Carter G. Woodson, pp. 65–73.

Suggested References

History of West Africa, by Basil Davidson, pp. 19–130.

For More Extensive Study

A Tropical Dependency, by Flora Shaw Lugard.
Great Rulers of the African Past, by L. Dobler & W. A. Brown.
History of West Africa, edited by J. F. Ajayi and Michael Crowder.

Twenty-first Session:

    1. The Significance of the Year 1492—The Historical Background to the Slave Trade.

Main References

African Glory, by J. C. deGraft-Johnson, pp. 153–165.
African Background Outlined, by Carter G. Woodson, 217–255.

Suggested References

Introduction to African Civilizations, by John G. Jackson, read the Introduction.

For More Extensive Study

Four Centuries of Portuguese Expansion, by C. R. Boxer.
The Horizon History of Africa, by Alvin M. Josephy, Jr.
A Tropical Dependency, by Flora Shaw Lugard.

Twenty-Second Session:

1. The Significance of the Year 1492: The Second Rise of Europe.
2. Gold as a Factor Before Slavery.
3. The Elmina Castle Incident: 1482.

Main References

Topics in West African History, by Adu Boahen, pp. 103–112.
African Glory, by J. C. deGraft-Johnson, pp. 120–126.

Suggested References

History of the African People, by Robert W. July, pp. 148–156.

For More Extensive Study

A History of the Gold Coast and Ashanti, by W. W. Claridge.
Ghana the Morning AFter, by K. Budu-Acquah.
Capitalism and Slavery, by Eric Williams.
Documents on West Indian History, by Eric Williams.

Twenty-Third Session:

1. How and Why the Slave Trade: The First Impact of the Portuguese.
2. African Reaction to the Portuguese.

Main References

African Glory, by J. C. deGraft-Johnson, pp. 127–133.
Topics in West African History, by Adu Boahen, pp. 103–112.

Suggested References

History of West Africa, by Basil Davidson, pp. 293–298.

For More Extensive Study

Black Mother: The Slave Trade, by Basil Davidson.
Slavery and Social Death, by Orlando Patterson.

Twenty-Fourth Session:

1. The Portuguese in the Congo.
2. The Failure of a Partnership—Why?
3. The Aftermath of the Failure.

Main References

A History of African People, by Robert W. July, pp. 148–156.

Suggested References

Portugal in Africa, by James Duffy, Penguin African Library, Baltimore, 1963, pp. 25–46.

For More Extensive Study

Four Centuries of Portuguese Expansion, by C. R. Boxer.
Daily Life in the Kingdom of the Kono, (From the 16th to the 18th Centuries), by George Balandier.
Political Awakening in the Belgian Congo, (The Politics of Fragmentation), by Rene Lemarchand.

Twenty-Fifth Session:

1. The Portuguese Conflict of Angola.
2. Encounter with Nzingha.
3. Nzingha's Resistance to Portuguese Rule.

Main References

African Glory, by J. C. deGraft-Johnson, pp. 254–290.

Suggested References

Portugal in Africa, by James Duffy, pp. 25–72.
Four Centuries of Portuguese Expansion, by C. R. Boxer.

For More Extensive Study

World's Great Men of Color, by J. A. Rogers.
The Portuguese Conquest of Angola, by David Birmingham.
Trade and Conflict in Angola, by David Birmingham.

Twenty-Sixth Session:

1. East African Slave Trade.
2. Islamic Rationale for the Slave Trade.
3. The Arab Treatment of the Slaves.

Main References

African Glory, by J. C. deGraft-Johnson, pp. 144–150.

Suggested References

A History of East and Central Africa, by Basil Davidson, pp. 112–144.
Portugal in Africa, by James Duffy, pp. 25–72.

For More Extensive Study

The General History of Africa, Vol. 7, UNESCO.
Documents II: Slavery in the Indian Ocean, UNESCO.

Twenty-Seventh Session:

1. African Slave Trade and the Settlement of the New World.
2. Africa Before the Atlantic Slave Trade.
3. Arab Slave Trade as Preface to the Atlantic Slave Trade.

Main References

History of the African People, by Robert W. July, pp. 148–168.
Africa in History, by Basil Davidson, pp. 60–94.

Suggested References

History of West Africa, by J. D. Fage, pp. 111-132.

For More Extensive Study

Capitalism and Slavery, by Eric Williams.
The Sociology of Slavery, by Orlando Patterson.
The General History of Africa, Chapter 7, UNESCO.

Twenty-Eighth Session:

1. The Collapse of Western Sudan.
2. The Politics of Morocco Before the Invasion.
3. The Invasion Itself.
4. The Aftermath.

Main References

Topics in West African History, by Adu Boahen, pp. 32-37.
A History of the African People, by Robert W. July, pp. 63-69.
Introduction to African Civilizations, by John G. Jackson.

Suggested References

Introduction to African Civilizations, by John G. Jackson, pp. 296-360.

For More Extensive Study

The Lost Cities of Africa, by Basil Davidson.
Realm of the Evening Star: Morocco and the Land of the Moors, by Eleanor Hoffman.
Timbuctoo the Mysterious, by Felix DuBois.

Twenty-Ninth Session:

1. Africa and the World, 1600 A.D.

Thirtieth Session: Seminar: Review of all Previous Sessions.

AFRICA: ITS PLACE IN WORLD HISTORY FROM 1600 A.D. TO THE PRESENT

SECTION TWO

This guide is designed as an introduction to the history of modern Africa. It is Part II of a survey of African history that began with African history from the origin of man to 1600 A.D.

RATIONALE

This guide is a general survey of African history and its relationship to the history of the rest of the world. The guide will emphasize an Afro-centric point of view, using a large number of books and documents by Europeans which tend to prove that the generally accepted European view of African history and African civilizations is wrong. This view of the African people and African civilizations is wrong. This view of the African people was created to justify the slave trade and the colonial system. I have also used a large number of books and documents prepared by African writers and writers of African descent in the United States and in the West Indies.

Further, in the presentation of this guide, I intend to prove that an Afro-centric view of history is academically defendable. In this case, it is mainly the view of the victim of its distortion. The restoration of African history and civilization as a part of world history and civilization is a meaningful contribution to future human relations.

RELEVANCE FOR STUDENTS

In this guide the students will be participating in an examination of the prefaces to modern African history. They will be exposed to a large number of references and documents, good and bad. Further, they will examine the events and personalities that shaped African history and be able to see that these events are current in many ways. The period covered by the guide will afford the student the opportunity to learn how the slave system evolved into the colonial system and how the labor of the Africans and Asians helped to develop the economic system called capitalism. The admission or denial of African history was a major factor in this protracted crime against most of mankind.

First Session:

1. The impact of the Moroccan invasion on the cultural life of Songhay and its effect on West Africa in general.
2. The nature of the resistance to Moroccan rule during the occupation of the Western Sudan.
3. The intellectual destruction of the Western Sudan— The exiling of the scholars.

Main References

Topics in West African History, by Adu Boahen, pp. 13–21.
Dawn of African History, by Roland Oliver, pp. 60–67.

Suggested References

Ancient African Kingdoms, by Margaret Shinnie, pp. 43–66.
History of West Africa, vol. 1, edited by J. F. Ade Ajayi and Michael Crowder, pp. 441–483.

The Horizon History of Africa, edited by Alvin M. Josephy, Jr., pp. 359–464.

For More Extensive Study

Lost Cities of Africa, by Basil Davidson.
History of West Africa, Vol. I & II, by J. F. Ade Ajayi and Michael Crowder.
Timbuctoo the Mysterious, by Felix DuBois.

Second Session:

1. Commercial Trading Before the Slave Trade.
2. The Troubled Years of African Civilization—The First Impact of the Slave Trade.
3. African Reaction to the Slave Trade and the Coming of the Europeans.

Main References

African Background Outlined, by Carter G. Woodson, pp. 217–225.
African Glory, by J. C. deGraft-Johnson, pp. 151–165.

Suggested References

A History of West Africa, by Basil Davidson, pp. 293–298.
The Horizon History of Africa, edited by Alvin M. Josephy,Jr., pp. 304–351 and 352–399.

For More Extensive Study

Topics in West African History, by Adu Boahen, see chapter: "The Coming of the Europeans."
Black Mother: The African Slave Trade: Pre-Colonial History 1450–1850, by Basil Davidson.

Capitalism and Slavery, by Eric Williams.

Third Session:

1. The Slave Trade and Competition Among European Nations for Areas of Influence in Africa.
2. The Slave Trade and the Origins of African Underdevelopment.
3. The Slave Trade and the Destruction of African Culture and Images.

Main References

Topics in West African History, by Adu Boahen, pp. 103–133.
African Glory, by J. C. deGraft-Johnson, pp. 151–165.
How Europe Underdeveloped Africa, by Walter Rodney, pp. 40–124.
The Slave Trade and Slavery, edited by John Henrik Clarke and Vincent Harding, pp. 10–21.

Suggested References

African Mother: The Slave Trade, by Basil Davidson.

For More Extensive Study

The Horizon History of Africa, by Alvin M. Josephy, Jr.
History of West Africa, by J. F. Ade Ajayi & Michael Crowder.

Fourth Session:

1. Nations and Civilizations of the Congo and Southwest Africa: The Struggle Against the Portuguese Influence.

2. The Portuguese in Mbundu, That Later Became Angola.
3. The Aftermath of the Partnership That Failed.

Main References

World's Great Men of Color, by J. A. Rogers, Vol. 1, pp. 247–250.
The Destruction of Black Civilizations, by Chancellor Williams, pp. 157–171.

Suggested References

The Horizon History of Africa, edited by Alvin M. Josephy, Jr., pp. 365–367.
The Dawn of African History, edited by Roland Oliver, pp. 69–75.
Portugal in Africa, by James Duffy, pp. 25–46.

For More Extensive Study

Four Centuries of Portuguese Expansion, by C. R. Boxer.
The Portuguese Conquest of Angola, by David Birmingham.
Trade and Conflict in Angola.

Fifth Session:

1. Nations and Civilizations of East and Central Africa—The Pre-Colonial Period.
2. The Coming of the Portuguese to East Africa.
3. Arab-Portuguese Partnership in the Slave Trade.

Main References

How Europe Underdeveloped Africa, by Walter Rodney, pp. 103–261.

African Glory, by J. C. deGraft-Johnson, pp. 144–150.

Suggested References

The Horizon History of Africa, edited by Alvin M. Josephy, Jr., pp. 368–371.
History of East and Central Africa, by Basil Davidson, pp. 1–56.

For More Extensive Study

The Cambridge History of East Africa, edited by Roland Oliver
The General History of Africa, Vol. VII., UNESCO.
UNESCO Document II: Slavery in the Indian Ocean.

Sixth Session:

1. The Formation of Nations in Southern Africa from the Death of Shaka to the Last Zulu War in Natal, 1906.
2. The Zulus After the Death of Shaka.

Main References

African Heroes and Heroines, by Carter G. Woodson, pp. 148–166.
World's Great Men of Color, by J. A. Rogers, pp. 265–275, 287–293 and 363–369.

For More Extensive Study

The Zulu Aftermath, by J. Omar-Cooper.
Emperor Shaka the Great, by Mazisi Kunene.
The Zulu Kings, by Brian Roberts.
Shaka, King of the Zulus, by Daniel Cohen.
Amazulu, by Thomas B. Jenkinson.

Seventh Session:

1. The People of Ghana from the Rise of the Ashanti During the Reign of Osei Tutu, Early in the 18th Century to the Exiling of King Prempah in 1896.
2. The People of Ghana from 1896 (The year King Prempah was exiled) to 1900 When the Yaa Asantewa Led the Ashanti People in the Last of the Ashanti Wars.
3. The Culture Consequence of the Ashanti War.

Main References

Topics in West African History, by Adu Boahen, pp. 53-76.
An Active History of Ghana, Book I & II, by Godfrey N. Brown and Philip M. Amonoo.
Ghana: A Historical Interpretation, by J. D. Fage.
The Ashanti of Ghana, by Sonia Bleeker.
Ghana: End of an Illusion, by Bob Fitch and Mary Oppenheimer.
Ancient Ghana and Mali, by Nehemia Levtzion.

Suggested References

A History of West Africa, by Basil Davidson, pp. 129-152.
World's Great Men of Color, by J. A.Rogers, pp. 142-144 and 254-263.
Ashanti Heroes, by K. O. Bonsu Kveretwie, pp. 50-54.

For More Extensive Study

A History of the Gold Coast and Ashanti, by W. W. Claridge.
A History of the Gold Coast and Asante, by Carl S. Reindorf.

Gold Coast Native Institutions, by E. Casey Hayford.
Fanti Customary Lore, by John Mensah Sarbah.

Eighth Session:

1. The People of Nigeria: Culture and Transition on the
   North from the Collapse of the Western Sudan to the
   End of the Fulani Wars.
2. The Impact of the Fulani Wars on Northern Nigeria.
3. Culture and Religion in Conflict.

Main References

Topics in West African History, by Adu Boahen, pp. 33–
28 and 90–94.
The African Genius, by Basil Davidson, pp. 279–287.

Suggested References

Growth of African Civilization: The Revolutionary Years,
by Webster, et al, pp. 3–14.
The Horizon History of Africa, edited by Alvin M. Josephy, Jr.

For More Extensive Study

A History of Modern Nigeria, by Michael Crowder.
The Sword of Truth: The Life of Usman, by Dan Fodio.

Ninth Session:

1. The People of Nigeria: Culture and Transition
   Among the Yorubas and the Eboes in the 19th
   Century.
2. The Career of Jaja and the Start of Nigerian
   Nationalism.
3. The Politics of Exile in Nigeria.

Main References

Topics in West African History, by Adu Boahen, pp. 90-94.

Suggested References

A History of West Africa, by Basil Davidson, pp. 135-146.
A Thousand Years of West African History, by J. F. Ade Ajayi and Espiel Ian, pp. 186-200.
The Horizon History of Africa, edited by Alvin M. Josephy, Jr. pp. 448-495.

For More Extensive Study

A History of West Africa, by Basil Davidson.
Trade and Politics in the Niger Delta, 1830-1885, by K. Omwuku Dike.
Revolution and Power Politics in Yorubaland, 1840-1893, by S. A. Akintoye.
Nigeria: Background to Nationalism, by James S. Coleman.

Tenth Session:

1. The People, the Cultures and the Resistance Movements in West Africa at the End of the 19th Century: Re: Samory Toure of Guinea and King Behazin of Dahomey.
2. The Beginning of a New Political Elite in West Africa.
3. The Politics of Exile.

Main References

Pan-Africanism or Communism, by George Padmore, pp. 54–101.
World's Great Men of Color, by J. A. Rogers, pp. 328–349.

Suggested References

Protest and Power in Black Africa, edited by Robert I. Rothberg and Ali A. Mazuri, pp. 37–80 and 512–571.

For More Extensive Study

Nigeria: Background to Nationalism, by James S. Coleman.
Trade and Politics in the Niger Delta, 1830–1885, by K. Onwuku Dike.
A History of Modern Nigeria, by Michael Crowder.

Eleventh Session:

1. Resistance Movements in the Sudan and Along the East Coast of Africa at the End of the 19th Century. The Mahdi (Mohammed Ahmed) Period in the Sudan and the Period of Sayed Mohammed Abdullah Hassen in Somalia.
2. Political Movements in East and in Central Africa.
3. The Role of Islam in East and Central African Revolts.

Main References

World's Great Men of Color, by J. A. Rogers, pp. 295–309.

Suggested References

World's Great Men of Color, by J. A. Rogers, pp. 178–183.

African Heroes and Heroines, by Carter G. Woodson, pp. 79–82

Tarikh, Vol. 1, No. 2: *African Leadership,* (read entirely)
Vol. 2, No. 3: *Six Aspects of African History* (read entirely)

For More Extensive Study

Fire and Sword in the Sudan, by Slatin Pasha.
A *Short History of the Sudan,* by Mandous el Mahdi.
The Fighting Sudanese, by H. C. Jackson.
A *History of the Sudan to 1821,* by A. J. Arkell.

Twelfth Session:

1. Africa at the End of the 19th Century: An Overview.
2. The Development of the South African National Congress and Other Non-Military Resistance Movements in Southern Africa.
3. The Birth of South African Trade Unionism.

Main References

Pan-Africanism or Communism, by George Padmore, pp. 268–357.
Topics in West African History, by Adu Boahen, pp. 146–155.
Tarikh, Vol. 1, No. 4: *Modernishers in Africa.*
Vol. 2, No. 2: *African Achievement and Tragedy.*
Vol. 2, No. 3: *Six Aspects of African History.*
Vol. 2, No. 4: *France in Africa.*

Suggested References

How Europe Underdeveloped Africa, by Walter Rodney, pp. 223–287.

For More Extensive Study

Time Longer Than Rope, by Robert Roux.

Thirteenth Session:

1. The 20th Century Consequences of the So-Called "Scramble for Africa."
2. The Consequences of the So-Called "Scramble" in Other Parts of Africa.
3. Was this the Beginning or the End of the Scramble for Africa?

Main References

The Destruction of Black Civilizations, by Chancellor Williams, pp. 207–222.
Pan-Africanism or Communism, by George Padmore, pp. 164–204.

Suggested References

How Europe Underdeveloped Africa, by Walter Rodney, pp. 261–287.

For More Extensive Study

The Black Man's Burden, by E. D. Morel.
King Leopold's Congo, by Ruth Slade.
King Leopold's Rule in Africa, by E. D. Morel.
Red Rubber, by E. D. Morel.

Fourteenth Session:

1. The Rise of Political Movements in Africa.
2. The Impact of the First World War on Africa.
3. Colonialism and Contradiction.

Main References

Pan-Africanism or Communism, by George Padmore, pp. 54–115.
How Europe Underdeveloped Africa, by Walter Rodney, pp. 223–287.

Suggested References

Africans and Their History, by Joseph E. Harris, pp. 138–182.

For More Extensive Study

History of West Africa, Vols. I & II, by J. F. Ajayi.
Renascent Africa, by Nnamdi Azikiwe.

Fifteenth Session:

1. The Independence Explosion and the Impact of Africa on Our Time.
2. The Consequences of the Explosion Within Africa.
3. The Consequences of the Explosion Abroad.
4. The Consequences of the Explosion on the Economy of Europe.

Main References

Africa Must Unite, by Kwame Nkrumah.
Ghana: The Autobiography of Kwame Nkrumah by Kwame Nkrumah.
Neo-Colonialism, the Last Stage of Imperialism, by Kwame Nkrumah.

Suggested References

Which Way Africa, by Basil Davidson.

Can Africa Survive, by Basil Davidson.
Report on Southern Africa, by Basil Davidson.
The African Awakening, by Basil Davidson.

For More Extensive Study

The First Dance of Freedom, by Martin Meredith.
Marcus Garvey and the Vision of Africa, edited by John
Henrik Clarke.
Dark Days in Ghana, by Kwame Nkrumah.

*Sixteenth Session: A Seminar: Africa Here and Now. Main
References*

Africans and their History, by Joseph E. Harris, pp. 133–216.
Pan-Africanism or Communism, by George Padmore, pp.
268–418.

Suggested References

Current newspapers and magazine articles about Africa.

AFRICA: ITS PLACE IN WORLD HISTORY
AFRICAN-AMERICAN HISTORY— FROM SLAVERY TO EMANCIPATION

SECTION THREE

This reading guide was developed as a survey of the historical experiences of the African people in the United States from the pre-Columbian presence to the period of the Reconstruction, beginning with the African background. This is the first part of a two-part reading guide designed for undergraduates and teachers.

ACADEMIC OBJECTIVE

The intent of this reading guide is to examine, in detail, the role that the people of African descent have played in the making of the nations in what is called the "New World." Considerable time will be used to show that all the Africans who were brought to the "New World" were not slaves. In fact, some were explorers, paid sailors and soldiers, freebooters and skilled craftsmen.

Further, it will be shown that the forced labor of the Africans helped to lay the basis for the economic system called capitalism. These Africans have always been a part of "New World" history and are now a determining factor in that history.

This reading guide will reveal that the phrase, "New World" is highly questionable in the light of the old and new evidence that tends to prove that people of African descent were in large parts of North and South America and the Caribbean Islands long before Christopher Columbus opened up this part of the world for European settlement. This reading guide is presented from an Afro- centric point of view, using mainly the books and documents of writers of African descent in all cases where this material is available.

New information, by both Black and White writers, that proves beyond question, that people of African descent have had a pre- Columbian presence in what is called the "New World," will be introduced into the reading guide. Such new work as: *Introduction to African Civilizations*, by John G. Jackson, (1970) and *The Art of Terracotta Pottery in pre-Columbian Central and South America*, by Alexander Von Wuthenau, (1965) will be examined with students' participation. In depth magazine articles on this subject, such as, *"The Beginning of the African Diaspora: Black Men in Ancient and Medieval America,"* parts I & II, by Legrand H. Clegg, (in a *Bibliography on African Affairs*, Vol. 2, Nos. 11 and 12, November and December, (1969), will also be examined. A comparison will be made between these works and an earlier study of this subject by Professor Leo Wiener in his massive three volumes of research entitled, *Africa and the Discovery of America*, (1920).

By making a more creative use of new and old material, and looking at history from the vantage of the victims of European expansion into what they call the "New World," this reading guide will examine the dimensions and significance of the impact of the Africans on the nations, civilizations and cultural life of North and South America.

ACADEMIC NEED

African-American history is an important part of the history of the United States and the settlement of what is referred to as the "New World." This reading guide is designed for any student who wishes to make a serious study of this subject and is prepared to do the extensive reading required. In my opinion, if African- American history is important enough to be read by any student, it is important enough to be read by all students.

TEACHING METHODOLOGY

This reading guide will develop the subjects of the session and place them in proper perspective so that a meaningful discussion can follow among the students and the instructor. In these discussions, the subject will be viewed from many sides, and a comparison will be made between what the instructor has said and what was written in the required and general reference relating to the subject.

First Session:

1. The African Basis of World History.
2. West African Coastal States During the Early Part of the 15th Century.
3. European Positive Entry and Negative Results.

Main References

Before the Mayflower, by Lerone Bennett, Jr., pp. 3–28.
America's Black Past, edited by Eric Foner, pp. 1–27.

Suggested References

Breaking the Chains of Bondage, by Norman E. W. Hodges, pp. 1–24.
The Negro, by W. E. B. DuBois, Chapters 1–4, pp. 5–35.
Topics in West African History, by Adu Boahen, pp. 3–28.
The Chronological History of the Negro in America, edited by Peter M. Bergman and Mort N. Bergman, pp. 1–9.

A *People Uprooted 1500–1800*, edited by Benjamin Quarles and Sterling Stuckey, pp. 7–35.

For More Extensive Study

The Horizon History of Africa, edited by Alvin M. Josephy, Jr.
West Africa, by J. F. Ajayi.
A *History of West Africa to the 19th Century*, by Basil Davidson and F. K. Bush.

Second Session:

1. How and Why African People were Lost from the Pages of World History.
2. The European Control of Image.
3. The European Control of the Concept of God.

Main References

The Slave Trade and Slavery, edited by John Henrik Clarke and Vincent Harding, pp. 1–9.
A *People Uprooted 1500–1800. Vol. 1*, edited by Benjamin Quarles and Sterling Stuckey, pp. 6–69.

Suggested References

The Negro in Our History, by Carter G. Woodson and Charles H. Wesley, pp. 1–52.
The Chronological History of the Negro in America, edited by Peter M. Bergman and Mort N. Bergman, pp. 1–31.

For More Extensive Study

How Europe Underdeveloped Africa, by Walter Rodney.
The Betrayal of the Negro, by Rayford Logan.
Up From Slavery, by Booker T. Washington.

Third Session:

1. The Slave Trade Begins.
2. The Role the Africans Played or Did Not Play in the Slave Trade.
3. The Slave Trade in the Economic Recovery of Europe.

Main References

The Slave Trade and Slavery, edited by John Henrik Clarke and Vincent Harding, pp. 1-9.
The Negro in the Making of America, by Benjamin Quarles, pp. 15-32.
Pioneers and Planters: Black Beginnings in America, by Joseph E. Penn *and* Earl E. Thorpe, pp. 3-11.

Suggested References

Capitalism and Slavery, by Eric Williams, pp. 3-29.
How Europe Underdeveloped Africa, by Walter Rodney, pp. 84-101.

For More Extensive Study

The Shaping of Black America, by Lerone Bennett, Jr.
Before the Mayflower, by Lerone Bennett, Jr.
Long Memory: the Black Experience in America, by Mary Frances Berry and John W. Blassingame.

Fourth Session:

1. The Impact of the Africans on the "New World," Part 1, the Pre-Columbian Presence.
2. New Books and New Theories on the Pre-Columbian Presence of Africans in the Americas.

3. The Economic Factor of the Presence of the Africans in America.

Main References

From Slavery to Freedom, by John Hope Franklin, pp. 3–10.
The Slave Trade and Slavery, edited by John Henrik Clarke and Vincent Harding, pp. 10–17.

Suggested References

Introduction to African Civilizations, by John G. Jackson, pp. 232–260.

For More Extensive Study

They Came Before Columbus, by Ivan van Sertima.
World's Great Men of Color, vol. II, by J. A. Rogers.
The Negro in Our History, by Carter G. Woodson.

Fifth Session:

1. The Impact of the Africans on the "New World," Part II, the African Explorers.
2. The Africans in the "New World" Who Were Not Slaves.

Main References

The Slave Trade and Slavery, edited by John Henrik Clarke and Vincent Harding, pp. 10–32.
Capitalism and Slavery, by Eric Williams, pp. 3–29.

Suggested References

Before the Mayflower, by Lerone Bennett, Jr., pp. 3–47.

Pioneers and Planters: Black Beginnings in America, by
Joseph E. Penn and Earl E. Thorpe, last three chapters.
Blacks in America: Then and Now, by Edgar A. Tappin,
pp. 1–8
Great Negroes Past and Present, by Russell L. Adams, pp.
15–16.

For More Extensive Study

The Slave Community, by John W. Blassingame.
There is a River, by Vincent Harding.
Long Memory: the Black Experience in America, by Mary
Frances Berry and John W. Blassingame.

Sixth Session:

1. The Impact of the Africans on the "New World," Part
   III, Extension of the Slave Trade.
2. The Scramble for White Labor in Europe. The Conditions Behind the Scramble. What Europeans Were Being Enslaved, How and Why.

Main References

The Slave Trade and Slavery, edited by John Henrik
Clarke and Vincent Harding, pp. 1–18.
A People Uprooted 1500–1800, edited by Benjamin
Quarles and Sterling Stuckey, pp. 37–44.

Suggested References

Capitalism and Slavery, by Eric Williams, pp. 3–50.
Early America 1492–1812, by William Loren Katz, pp. 1–
7.

For More Extensive Study

The Shaping of Black America, by Lerone Bennett, Jr., Chapters I and II.
Slavery and Social Death, by Orlando Patterson.

Seventh Session:

1. Red Servitude, Black Servitude, the Destruction of the Indians and their Replacement by the Africans.
2. The Distribution of the (so-called) Indians. A Further Preparation for the Extension of the African Slave Trade.
3. Slavery and the Planting of American Racism.

Main References

Pioneers and Planters: Black Beginnings in America, by Joseph E. Penn and Earl E. Thorpe, pp. 3–17.
The Chronological History of the Negro in America, by Peter M. Bergman and Mort N. Bergman, pp. 1–13.
A People Uprooted 1500–1800, edited by Benjamin Quarles and Sterling Stuckey, pp. 37–51.

Suggested References

Early America 1492–1812, by William Loren Katz, pp. 1–11.
The Shaping of Black America, by Lerone Bennett, Jr., pp. 61–80.
History of Black Americans, by Philip S. Foner, pp. 95–113.

For More Extensive Study

The Slave Community, by John Blassingame.
Slavery and the Period of Revolution, by David Brian.
Slavery and Western Civilization.

From Columbus to Castro: The History of the Caribbean,
by Eric Williams.

Eighth Session:

1. 1619 and the Beginning of Black Slavery in the United
   States. What Manner of Slavery Was This?
2. The Slavery System Developed Slowly. Why?
3. White Servitude: A Neglected Factor in Slavery.

Main References

Before the Mayflower, by Lerone Bennett, Jr., pp. 29–74.
America's Black Past, edited by Eric Foner, pp. 50–74.
From Slavery to Freedom, by John Hope Franklin, pp. 40–
59.

Suggested References

America's Black Past, edited by Eric Foner, pp. 75–111.
The Shaping of Black America, by Lerone Bennett, Jr.,
pp. 61–80.
The Slave Community, by John H. Blassingame, pp. 1–
40.

For More Extensive Study

The Burden of Southern History, by C. Vann Woodward.
The Mind of the South, by Wilbur Joseph Cash.

Ninth Session:

1. American Independence and American Slavery After
   the Revolution.
2. The Founding Fathers: Did they Really Mean What
   they Said?
3. Liberty, Death and Slavery.

Main References

From Slavery to Freedom, by John Hope Franklin, pp. 126–144.
Before the Mayflower, by Lerone Bennett, Jr., pp. 108–125.
Capitalism and Slavery, by Eric Williams, pp. 48–69.

Suggested References

Black Protest, by Joanne Grant, pp. 17–30.
A People Uprooted 1500–1800, edited by Benjamin Quarles and Sterling Stuckey, pp. 85–109.

For More Extensive Study

Pioneers in Protest, by Lerone Bennett, Jr.
Prince Hall and the African Lodge, by Charles Wesley.
A History of the Negro Race in the United States, vol. 1, by George Washington Williams.

Tenth Session:

1. The Impact of the Haitian Revolution on the Slave Systems of the New World.
2. The Aftermath of the Haitian Revolution.
3. Slave Sailors and the News of the Haitian Revolution.

Main References

The Black Jacobins, by C. L. R. James, pp. 145–198.
Before the Mayflower, by Lerone Bennett, Jr., pp. 96–126.

Suggested References

The Negro, by W. E. B. DuBois, pp. 96–109.

Chains of Slavery 1800–1865, edited by Benjamin Quarles and Sterling Stuckey, pp. 7–33.

For More Extensive Study

Black Abolitionists, by Benjamin Quarles.
The Negro in the American Revolution, by Benjamin Quarles.
The Negro in Our History, by Carter G. Woodson.

Eleventh Session:

1. Resistance Movements in the First Half of the 19th Century: The Massive Slave Revolts.
2. The "Free" Blacks in New England and in the Abolitionist Movement.

Main References

Before the Mayflower, by Lerone Bennett, Jr., pp. 127–159.
From Slavery to Freedom, by John Hope Franklin, pp. 242–250.

Suggested References

American Negro Slave Revolts, by Herbert Aptheker, pp. 162–208.
Black Protest, by Joanne Grant, pp. 31–62.
The Hurricane of Promise, by Raymond McHugh, pp. 3–21.
Blacks in America: Then and Now, by Edgar A. Tappin, pp. 9–16.

For More Extensive Study

Pioneers in Protest, by Lerone Bennett, Jr.

The Black Abolitionists, by Benjamin Quarles.
The Life and Times of Frederick Douglass, by Frederick Douglass.

Twelfth Session:

1. The Impact of David Walker's Appeal on the Thought and Action of the Abolitionists' Movement After 1829.
2. The David Walker Era.
3. David Walker's Appeal as Literature.

Main References

Pioneers in Protest, by Lerone Bennett, Jr., pp. 69–82.

Suggested References

The Continual Cry of David Walker, by Herbert Aptheker.
David Walker's Appeal, Introduction by David Wiltse.
Chronicles of Negro Protest, by Bradford Chambers, pp. 65–75.
The Hurricane Promise: Free Negroes Before the Civil War, by Raymond McHugh, pp. 15–47.

For More Extensive Study

Great Negroes Past and Present, by Russell Adams.
Martin Delaney: Father of Black Nationalism, by Dorothy Sterling.

Thirteenth Session:

1. The Impact of the Black Elite on the Abolitionists' Movement. (i.e., Frederick Douglas, John Russwurm,

Samuel Ringgold Ward, Samuel Cornish and Henry Highland Garnett.

2. The Impact of the African Colonization Society on Social Thought Relating to Black Americans.

Main References

Pioneers in Protest, by Lerone Bennett, Jr., pp. 59–197.
The Negro in the Making of America, by Benjamin Quarles, pp. 83–108.

Suggested References

Chronicles of Negro Protest, by Bradford Chambers, pp. 76– 121.
Rebellion and Protest: The Anti-Slavery Crusade, by Fern Kelly, pp. 21–32.
Chains of Slavery 1800–1865, edited by Benjamin Quarles and Sterling Stuckey, pp. 61–113.

For More Extensive Study

The Slave Community, by John W. Blassingame.
The Black Abolitionists, by Benjamin Quarles.
William Styron's Nat Turner: Ten Black Writers Respond, edited by John Henrik Clarke.
Long Memory: The Black Experience In America, by Mary F. Berry & John W. Blassingame.

AFRICA: ITS PLACE IN WORLD HISTORY FROM THE RECONSTRUCTION TO THE PRESENT

SECTION FOUR

The following pages provide detailed survey of the main events in African-American history from the period of the Reconstruction to the present. The intent of this reading guide is to show that the Civil War, the Reconstruction and its aftermath are pivotal events in American history whose reverberations still affect the political structure of America. Other major topics are:

Black America at the end of the 19th century
The Booker T. Washington Era
W. E. B. DuBois and the new Black Radical Elite
Black Americans in the First World War
The Rise and Fall of the Garvey Movement
Blacks in the Great Depression
Black Americans in the Second World War
The Rise of the Civil Rights and
    Black Power Movements after World War II

Because early African-American history is inseparable from African history, it is important for students to have at least a basic background knowledge of what happened in Africa before the slave trade. There is also an urgent need for simple and direct information on how and why the slave trade came. For that reason, I have included a number of books on the suggested reading list that deal with the African background and the relationship African History has to both African-American history and world history in general.

I particularly call your attention to the following books which are essential for this background. Among them are the reissues of "The Negro," by W. E. B. DuBois, which are especially important; combined with Dr. Boahen's "Topics in West African History." These provide a good overview of West Africa prior to and after the start of the slave trade. "African Background Outlined" by Carter G. Woodson, gives a world view of the African people before and after this greatest of human tragedies.

First Session:

1. The Civil War, Emancipation, the New Freedom and New Illusions: Black Political Power Brief and Fleeting to 1875.
2. Background of the Conflict: What was the North Fighting For? What was the South fighting for? Why was the issue of slavery so easily lost as a cause for this conflict?
3. Black Soldiers in the Civil War: Who were they and why did they fight?

Second Session:

1. President Lincoln and the Civil War: The Second Phase.

Main References

The Betrayal of the Negro, by Rayford Logan, pp. 11–23.
Before the Mayflower, by Lerone Bennett, Jr., pp. 160–219.

Suggested References

Negro Social and Political Thought, by Howard Brotz, pp. 226–297.
Forward to Freedom, Mr. Lincoln and the Negroes, by Grassie H. Hudson, pp. 3–37.

For More Extensive Study

Black Reconstruction, by W. E. B. DuBois.
Emancipation, by John Hope Franklin.
The Burden of Southern History, by C. Vann Woodward.

Third Session:

1. Reconstruction: Black Political Ascending: A Short Day in the Sun.

Fourth Session:

1. Reconstruction: The Last Phase.

Main References

Black Power U.S.A., by Lerone Bennett, Jr.
Before the Mayflower, by Lerone Bennett, Jr., pp. 127–219.

Suggested References

The Betrayal of the Negro, by Rayford Logan, pp. 11–23.
The Lost Promise—Reconstruction in the South, by Dr. W. Sherman Jackson, pp. 3–19.
Black Reconstruction in America 1860–1880, by W.E.B. DuBois.

For More Extensive Study

The Burden of Southern History, by C. Vann Woodward.

Emancipation, by John Hope Franklin.
The World the Slaves Made, by Eugene Genovese.
The Slave Community, by John Blassingame.

Fifth Session:

1. The Betrayal of the Reconstruction and the Emergence of the Booker T. Washington Era.

Sixth Session:

1. Black Politicians and their White "Allies."

Main References

The Betrayal of the Negro, by Rayford Logan, pp. 165–313.
Before the Mayflower, by Lerone Bennett, Jr. pp. 228–274.
From Slavery to Freedom, by John Hope Franklin, pp. 297–323.

Suggested References

Pioneers in Protest, by Lerone Bennett, Jr., pp. 102–114.
The Lost Promise—Reconstruction in the South, by Dr. W. Sherman Jackson, pp. 7–47.
Separate and Unequal, edited by Benjamin Quarles and Sterling Stuckey, pp. 6–36.

For More Extensive Study

The Reconstruction, by W. E. B. DuBois.
Thee is a River, by Vincent Harding.
A History of the Negro Race in the United States, vols. I & II, by George Washington Williams.

Seventh Session:

1. The Making of Black Institutions Before and After the Betrayal of the Reconstruction.

Eighth Session:

1. The Booker T. Washington Era.

Main References

Pioneers in Protest, by Lerone Bennett, Jr., pp. 274–322.
From Slavery to Freedom, by John Hope Franklin, pp. 389–449.

Suggested References

The Negro Vanguard, by Richard Bardolph, pp. 55–195.
Negro Makers of History, by Carter G. Woodson and Charles Wesley, pp. 260–335.
Booker T. Washington and his Critics, published by Heath.
Up From Slavery, by Booker T. Washington.
The Reign of Jim Crow—Separatism and the Black Response, by Dr. Robert E. Moran.
Souls of Black Folks, by W. E. B. DuBois.
Black Titan: W. E. B. DuBois, by John Henrik Clarke, Beacon Press, 1970.

For More Extensive Study

Black Exodus, by Edwin S. Redkey.
Men of Mark, by William J. Simmons.
The Life and Times of Booker T. Washington, by Louis Hollins.

Ninth Session:

1. Black America Enters the Twentieth Century: New
Dreams and New Illusions.

Main References

From Slavery to Freedom, by John Hope Franklin, pp.
382-433.
American Negro, Old World Background, New World Experience, by Logan and Cohen, Chapter 7, *pp. 153-182.*

Suggested References

Black Exodus, by Edwin S. Redkey, pp. 1-46.
Northward Bound—From Sharecropping to City Living,
by Dr. Oscar E. Williams, pp. 3-18.

For More Extensive Study

Out of the House of Bondage, by Kelley Miller.
Souls of Black Folks, by W. E. B. DuBois.
The Gift of Black Folk, by W. E. B. DuBois.
The Burden of Southern History, by C. Vann Woodward.
The Strange Career of Jim Crow, by C. Vann Woodward.
The Rise and Fall of "Jim Crow," 1865-1964, by Frank
B. Latham.

Tenth Session:

1. W. E. B. DuBois and the New Black Leadership: A
Challenge to the Booker T. Washington Era.

Eleventh Session:

1. Pan-African Nationalism and Survival.

Main References

Black Exodus, by Edwin S. Redkey, pp. 252–310.
From Slavery to Freedom, by John Hope Franklin, pp. 546–576.

Suggested References

Black Protest, by Joanne Grant, latter part of the book.
From Slavery to Freedom, by John Hope Franklin, pp. 433–452.
Before the Mayflower, by Lerone Bennett, Jr., pp. 274–327.

For More Extensive Study

Pan-Africanism or Communism?, by George Padmore.
Pan-Africanism: A Brief History of an Idea in the African World, by John Henrik Clarke.
Long Memory—The Black Experience in America, by Mary Frances Berry and John Blassingame.

Twelfth Session:

1. Black America in the First World War.

Thirteenth Session:

1. Black Exodus 1915–1920.

Main References

From Slavery to Freedom, by John Hope Franklin, pp. 333–353.
Black America, by Eric Foner, pp. 324–348.

For More Extensive Study

Anyplace But Here, by Arna Bontemps.

Black Migration: Movement North 1900–1920, by Florette Henri.

Fourteenth Session:

1. Marcus Garvey and Black Nationalism.

Main References

From Slavery to Freedom, by John Hope Franklin, pp. 354–371.
Black Africa, by Eric Foner, pp. 349–370.

For More Extensive Study

Marcus Garvey and the Vision of Africa, by John Henrik Clarke.
The Garvey Papers, Vols. 1–5, edited by Robert Hill.
Garvey and Garveyism, edited by Amy Jacques Garvey.
Pan-Africanism or Communism?, by George Padmore.

Fifteenth Session:

1. The Harlem Renaissance.

Main References

From Slavery to Freedom, by John Hope Franklin, pp. 372–393.
Black America, by Eric Foner, pp. 371–387.

For More Extensive Study

The New Negro, by Alain Locke.
Voices from the Harlem Renaissance, by Nathan Irvin Huggins.

The Harlem Renaissance Remembered, by Arna Bontemps.

Sixteenth Session:

1. Blacks and the New Deal.

Main References

From Slavery to Freedom, by John Hope Franklin, pp. 394–413.
Black America, by Eric Foner, pp. 388–413.

For More Extensive Study

Negroes and the Great Depression, by Raymond Wolters.
The Bonus March, by Roger Daniels.
Hard Times, by Studs Terkel.

Seventeenth Session:

1. The Modern Civil Rights Era.

Main References

From Slavery to Freedom, by John Hope Franklin, pp. 394–413.
Black America, by Eric Foner, pp. 414–488.

For More Extensive Study

Black Protest, by Joanne Grant.
Stride Toward Freedom, by Martin Luther King, Jr.
Martin Luther King, Jr., by William Robert Miller.

Eighteenth Session:

1. Black Power.

Main References

From Slavery to Freedom, by John Hope Franklin, pp. 476–512.
Black America, by Eric Foner, pp. 482–556.

For More Extensive Study

The Negro Mood, by Lerone Bennett, Jr.
Pioneers in Protest, by Lerone Bennett, Jr.
Black Power, by Stokeley Carmichael and Charles Hamilton.

Nineteenth Session:

1. State of the Black Nation: The Present and Prospects for the Future—Class Discussion.

Twentieth Session:

1. Black History: An Aspect of Black Liberation.

Twenty-First Session:

1. New Directions in the Study of Black History: The Works of Lerone Bennett, Jr.—Part One.

Twenty-Second Session:

1. New Directions in the Study of Black History: Main Focus, *The Shaping of Black America,* by Lerone Bennett, Jr.

Twenty-Third Session:

1. Pan-Africanism Reconsidered.

Twenty-Fourth Session:

1. Black Americans and the Sixth Pan-African Congress.

Twenty-Fifth Session:

1. The Crisis of Black Leadership in America.

Twenty-Sixth Session:

1. The Crisis in Africa and in the Caribbean.

Twenty-Seventh Session:

1. The Changing Status of the Black Muslim Movement—Part One.

Twenty-Eighth Session:

1. The Changing Status of the Black Muslim Movement—Part Two.

Twenty-Ninth Session:

1. A World View of the Status of AFrican People.

Thirtieth Session:

1. Summary Session—Questions and Review.

Suggested Reading List and References

For this bibliography, I have selected what, in my opinion, are some of the best new books on African and African American history. I have purposely selected books that are easy to read and easy to obtain. Most of the books selected are in general circulation.

* An asterisk indicates that the book was written by an African or an African-American writer.

Adams, Russell L., *Great Negroes, Past and Present*, Afro-American Publishing Co., Chicago, 1966.

* Agebodeka, F., *The Rise of the Nation States: A History of the West African Peoples, 1600–1964*, Thomas Nelson and Sons, Ltd. London, 1965.

* Ajayi, J. F. A. and Crowder, Michael, editors, *History of West Africa*, Vols. I & II, Longman Group Ltd., London, 1971.

* ———, and Espie, Ian, editors, *A Thousand Years of West African History*, Ibadan University Press and Nelson, Copewood and Davis Streets, Camden, N.J., 1965.

* Akintoye, S. A., *Revolution and Power Politics in Yorubaland, 1840–1893*, Ibadan History Series, Humanities Press, New York, 1971.

American Heritage, editors, *Discoveries of the New World*, American Heritage Publishing, New York, 1965.

Aptheker, Herbert, *American Negro Slave Revolts*, International Publishers, New York, 1963.

———, *And Why Not Every Man?*. International Publishers, New York, 1970.

———, editor, *One Continual Cry by David Walker: Its Setting and Meaning*, Humanities Press, New York, 1965.

———, *The Negro People in America*, International Publishers, New York, 1946.

————, *The Negro in the American Revolution*, International Publishers, New York, 1940.

————, *Toward Negro Freedom*, New Century Publishers, New York, 1956.

————, *Essays in the History of the American Negro*, New World Paperback, New York, 1964.

————, *A Documentary History of the Negro People in the U.S.*, Vols. I & II, Citadel Press, New York, 1962.

* Asante, Molefi Kete and Asante, Kariamu Welsh, editors, *African Culture, The Rhythms of Unity*, Greenwood Press, Westport, Connecticut, 1985.

Arkell, A. J., *A History of the Sudan to 1821*, The Athlone Press, London, 1961.

* Azikiwe, Nnandi, *Renascent Africa*, Humanities Press, New York, 1968.

Balandier, Georges, *Daily Life in the Kingdom of the Kongo, From the Sixteenth to the Eighteenth Century*, Pantheon Books, New York, 1968.

Bardolph, Richard, *The Negro Vanguard*, Rinehart, New York., 1959.

Barth, Heinrich, *Travels and Discoveries in North and in Central Africa*, F. Cass, London, 1965.

* ben-Jochannan, Yosef, *African Origins of the Major "Western Religions"*, Alkebu-Ian Books, c/o Dr. Arthur Lewis, 725 St. Nicholas Ave., New York, 10030, 1970.

* ————, *Black Men of the Nile and His Family*, Alkebu-Ian Books, c/o Dr. Arthur Lewis, 725 St. Nicholas Ave., New York, 10030, 1972.

* ————, *Africa: Mother of Western Civilization*, Alkebu-Ian Books, c/o Dr. Arthur Lewis, 725 St. Nicholas Ave., New York, 10030, 1972.

* ————, with George E. Simmonds, *The Black Man's North and East Africa*, Alkebu-Ian Books, c/o Dr. Arthur Lewis, 725 St. Nicholas Ave., New York, 10030, 1971.

* ————, *Cultural Genocide in the Black and African Studies Curriculum*, Alkebu-Ian Books, 725 St. Nicholas Ave., New York, 10030, 1972.

* ——, *Africa: Mother of the Major Western Religions*, Alkebu- Ian Books, 725 St. Nicholas Ave., New York, 10030, 1970.

Benedict, Ruth, *Race: Science and Politics*, Viking Press, New York, 1964.

* Bennett, Lerone Jr., *The Negro Mood*, Penguin Press, Baltimore, 1966.

* ——, *Before the Mayflower: A History of Black America*, Johnson Publishing Co., Chicago, 1962.

* ——, *Pioneers in Protest*, Penguin Books, paperback, Baltimore, 1968.

* ——, *The Shaping of Black America*, Johnson Publishing Co., Chicago, 1975.

* ——, *Wade in the Water: Great Moments in Black History*, Johnson Publishing Co., Chicago.

* ——, *Black Power, U.S.A.*, Johnson Publishing Co., Chicago.

* ——, *Confrontation: Black and White*, Penguin Books, Baltimore, 1966.

Bergman, Peter M. and Bergman, Mort N., *The Chronological History of the Negro in America*, Mentor Books, New York, 1969.

* Berry, Mary Francis and Blassingame, John W., *Long Memory: The Black Experience in America*, Oxford University Press, New York.

Birmingham, David, *The Portuguese Conquest of Angola*, Oxford University Press, London, 1965.

——, *Trade and Conflict in Angola, The Mbundu and Their Neighbors Under the Influence of the Portuguese 1483–1790*, Clarendon Press, Oxford, 1966.

* Blassingame, John W., *The Slave Community: Plantation Life in the Ante-Bellum South*, Oxford University Press, New York.

Bleeker, Sonia, *The Ashanti of Ghana*, Dennis Dobson, London, 1966.

* Boahen, Adu with Ajayi, J. F. Ade and Tidy, Michael, *Topics* *in West African History*, Longman Group Ltd., Essex, England, 1986.

Bohannan, Paul and Curtin Phillip D., editors, *Africa and Africans*, The National History Press, New York, 1971.

* Bontemps, Arna, and Conroy, Jack, *Anyplace But Here*, Hill & Wang, New York, 1966.

* ———, *The Harlem Renaissance Remembered*, Dodd, Mead and Co., New York, 1972.

Boxer, C. R., *Four Centuries of Portuguese Expansion, 1415–1825: A Succinct Survey*, Witwatersrand University Press, Johannesburg, 1961.

* Bracey, John H. Jr., Meier, August & Rudwick, Elliott, editors, *Black Nationalism in America*, Bobbs-Merrill Co., Indianapolis, 1970.

Brawley, B., *A Social History of the American Negro*, Collier Books, New York, 1969.

Breasted, James Henry, *A History of Egypt*, Bantam Matrix Books, New York, 1967.

Brian, David, *Slavery and the Period of Revolution*, Cornell University Press, Ithaca.

———, *Slavery and Western Civilization*, Cornell University Press, Ithaca.

Brooks, Lester, *Great Civilizations of Ancient Africa*, Scholastic Books, New York.

Brotz, Howard, editor, *Negro Social & Political Thought, 1850–1920*, Basic Books, Inc., New York, 1966.

Brown, Godfrey N., *An Active History of Ghana*, Vol. I, - "From the Earliest Times to 1844, Vol. II—Since 1844, George Allen & Unwin Ltd., Great Britain, 1961 & 1964.

* Buah, F. K., *A New History for Schools and Colleges*, Book I & II, MacMillan and Co., New York.

* ———, *West Africa and Europe*, Book I & II, MacMillan and Co., New York.

* Budu-Acquah, K., *Ghana, The Morning After*, Goodwin Press, London, 1960.

Burke, Fred, edited and annotated, *Africa: Selected Readings,*

World Regional Studies, Houghton Mifflin Co., Burlington, Maine, paperback, 1965.

* Carmichael, Stokely and Hamilton, Charles, *Black Power: The Politics of Liberation,* Random House, New York, 1967.

* Cartey, Wilfred and Kilson, Martin, edited and Introduction, *The African Reader: Colonial Africa,* Random House-Vintage Books, paperback, New York, 1970.

Cash, Wilbur Joseph, *The Mind of the South,* Knopf Publishing Co., New York, 1941.

Chambers, Bradford, *Chronicles of Negro Protest,* Parents Magazine Press, 1968.

* Chijioke, F. A., *Beginning History of Ancient Africa,* Longmans Green and Co., Ltd., London, 1966.

Chu, Daniel and * Skinner, Elliott, A *Glorious Age in Africa, the Story of Three Great African Empires,* Zenith Books, Doubleday and Co., New York, 1965.

Clammer, David, *The Zulu War,* St. Martin Press, New York, 1973.

Claridge, W. W., A *History of the Gold Coast and Ashanti: From the Earliest Times to the Commencement of the Twentieth Century,* J. Murray, London, 1915.

Clark, J. Desmond, *The Prehistory of Africa,* Praeger Publishing Co., New York, 1970.

* Clarke, John Henrik, editor, *William Styron's Nat Turner: Ten Black Writers Respond,* Beacon Press, Boston, 1968.

* ——, *Pan-Africanism and the Liberation of Southern Africa: A Tribute to W. E. B. DuBois,* United Nations Center Against Apartheid and the African Heritage Studies Association, New York, 1978.

* ——, editor, *Marcus Garvey and the Vision of Africa,* Random House, New York, 1973.

* ——, with the editors of Freedomways, *Black Titan: W. E. B. DuBois,* an anthology, Beacon Press, Boston, 1970.

* ——, and Harding, Vincent, editors, *Slavery and the Slave Trade,* Holt, Rinehart and Winston, Inc., paperback, New York, 1970.

* ———, *The Lives of Great African Chiefs*, Pittsburgh Courier Publishing Co., Pittsburgh, 1958.

* ———, *History and Culture of Africa*, AEVAC Inc. Educational Publishers, Hempstead, New York, 1969.

* Clegg, Legrand H., *The Beginning of the African Diaspora: Black Men in Ancient and Medieval America*, Parts I & II, African Bibliographical Center, Washington, D.C.

Cohen, Daniel, *Shaka: King of the Zulus*, a biography, Doubleday and Co., New York, 1973.

Coleman, James S., *Nigeria, Background to Nationalism*, University of California Press, Berkeley, 1958.

Collins, Robert O., editor, *Problems in African History*, Prentice-Hall, Inc., Englewood Cliffs, N.J., 1968.

———, *African History: Text and Readings*, Random House, New York.

Cottrell, Leonard, *The Anvil of Civilization, Mentor: Ancient Civilizations*, New American Library, New York, 1957.

Crowder, Michael, *A Short History of Nigeria*, Praeger Publishing Co., New York, 1962.

Curtin, Phillip D., *African History*, American Historical Association, paperback pamphlet, Washington, D.C., 1967.

———, *Africa South of the Sahara*, Silver Burdett Co., paperback, Morristown, N.J., 1970.

Daniels, Roger, *The Bonus March, An Episode of the Great Depression*, Greenwood Publishing Corp., Westport, CT., 1971.

Davidson, Basil, *Black Mother: The Years of Our African Slave Trade: Pre-Colonial History, 1450–1850*, Atlantic-Little, Brown, Co., Boston, 1961.

———, *Which Way Africa? The Search for a New Society*, Penguin Books, Baltimore.

———, *Can Africa Survive?* Atlantic-Little, Brown & Co., Boston, 1974.

———, *Report on Southern Africa*, J. Cape, London, 1952.

———, *The African Awakening*, J. Cape, London, 1955.

———, *Discovering Our African Heritage*, Ginn and Co., paperback, Boston, 1970.

———, A History of East and Central Africa to the Late 19th Century, Anchor Books, Doubleday and Co., New York, 1969.

———, Africa in History, The MacMillan Co., New York, 1969.

———, A Guide to African History, Zenith Books, Doubleday and Co., New York, 1965.

———, The Lost Cities of Africa, an Atlantic Monthly Press Book by Little, Brown and Co., Boston, 1959.

———, The African Genius.

———, with Buah, F. K., A History of West Africa to the 19th Century, Anchor Books, Doubleday and Co., New York, 1966.

———, The Story of Africa, based on the Television Series, "AFRICA," a Mitchell Beazley production, London, 1984.

* deGraft-Johnson, J. C., African Glory, The Story of Vanished Negro Civilizations, George J. McLeod, Ltd., Toronto, 1954.

* Dike, K. Onwuka, Trade and Politics in the Niger Delta, 1830–1885, Clarendon Press, Oxford, England, 1956.

* Diop, Cheikh Anta, African Origins of Civilization: Myth or Reality, Lawrence Hill and Co., paperback, New York, 1974.

* ———, Civilization or Barbarism, Lawrence Hill & Co., New York, 1989.

* ———, A History of Pre-Colonial Africa, (in French) Presence Africaine, Paris, 1960.

* ———, The Origin of the Ancient Egyptians, pp. 27–57, article in"The Peopling of Ancient Egypt and the Deciphering of Meroitic Script," UNESCO's, The General History of Africa Studies and Documents, I, The General History of Africa Studies and Documents, II.

* Dobler, Larmia and Brown, William A., Great Rulers of the African Past, Zenith Books, Doubleday and Co., New York, 1965.

* Douglass, Frederick, Life and Times of Frederick Douglass, The Complete Autobiography, with a new Introduction by Rayford Logan, Collier Books, New York, 1962.

Drummer, Melvin, editor, *Black History*, Doubleday Anchor Books, New York.

* DuBois, W. E. B., *The Souls of Black Folk*, Crest Reprint, Fawcett Publications, 1965.

* ———, *Gifts of Black Folk*, Crest Reprint, Fawcett Publications, 1965.

* ———, *Black Reconstruction in America, 1860–1880*, Harcourt, Brace and Co., New York, 1935.

* ———, *The Negro*, Oxford University Press, New York, 1970.

* ———, *The World and Africa, An Inquiry Into the Part Which Africa Played in World History*, International Publishers, paperback, New York, 1965.

* ———, *The Suppression of the African Slave Trade to the U.S. of America, 1638–1870*, Schocken Books, New York, 1969.

Duffy, James, *Portugal in Africa*, Penguin African Library, Baltimore, 1963.

El Mahdi, Mandour, *A Short History of the Sudan*, Oxford University Press, New York, 1965.

* Essien-Udom, E.U., *Black Nationalism: A Search for An Identity in America*, Laurel Edition, Dell Publishing Co., New York, 1964.

Fage, J. D., *Ghana, A Historical Interpretation*, University of Wisconsin Press, Madison, WI, 1966.

———, *A History of West Africa*, Cambridge University Press, London, 1969.

Fairservis, Walter A., Jr., *The Ancient Kingdoms of the Nile*, Mentor Books, published by New American Library, paperback, New York, 1962.

* Fishel, Leslie and Quarles, Benjamin, *The Black American*, Oxford University Press, New York.

Fisher, Allan G. B. and Fisher, Humphrey J. *Slavery and Muslim Society in Africa, The Institution in Saharan and Sudanic Africa and the Trans-Saharan Trade*, Doubleday and Co., New York, 1971.

Fitch, Bob and Oppenheimer, Mary, *Ghana: End of an Illu-*

sion, Monthly Review Press, Vol. 18, No. 3, July–August, 1966, New York.

Foner, Eric, editor, *America's Black Past, A Reader in Afro-American History*, Harper and Row, New York, 1970.

Foner, Phillip S., *History of Black Americans*, Greenwich Press, Westport, CT.

Foster, William Z., *The Negro People in American History*, International Publishers, New York, 1970.

* Franklin, John Hope, *From Slavery to Freedom: A History of Negro Americans*, Alfred A. Knopf, New York, 1980.

———, *Emancipation*, Alfred A. Knopf, New York.

Freed, Rita E., *Ramses II, The Great Pharaoh and His Time*, Denver Museum of Natural History, Exhibition in the City of Denver, Memphis, TN, 1987.

Frye, J. D. ad Oliver, Roland, editors, *Papers in African Prehistory*, Cambridge University Press, New York, 1970.

Gabel, Creighton and Bennett, Norman, editors, *Reconstructing African Cultural History*, Boston University African Research Studies, No. 8, Boston, 1967.

Gailey, Harry A. Jr., *History of Africa From Earliest Times to 1800*, Holt, Rinehart and Winston, New York, 1970.

———, *History of Africa From 1900 to Present*, Holt, Rinehart and Winston, New York, 1970.

Gardiner, Alan, Sir., *Egypt of the Pharaohs*, A Galaxy Book, Oxford University Press, New York, 1966.

* Garvey, Amy Jacques, *Garvey and Garveyism*, Introduction by John Henrik Clarke, Collier Books, New York, 1970.

Genovese, Eugene, *The World the Slaveholders Made*, Vintage Books, New York, 1971.

Gossett, T. F., *Race: The History of an Idea in America*, Schocken Press, New York, 1965.

* Grant, Joanne, *Black Protest: History, Documents and Analyses, 1619 to the Present*, edited with Introduction and Commentary, Fawcett Premier Books, Greenwich, CT, 1968.

Graves, Anna Melissa, *Africa, the Wonder and the Glory*, Privately published, Baltimore, 1942.

———, editor, *Benvenuto Cellini: Had No Prejudice Against Bronze*, Waverly Press, Baltimore, 1942.

Greene, Lorenzo J., *The Negro in Colonial New England*, Columbia University Press, New York, 1942.

* Hansberry, William Leo, *Africa's Golden Past*, articles published in "Ebony Magazine:"

  1. *Life Could Have Begun in Kush*, Nov. 1964.
  2. *Historical Facts Challenge Notion that Christianity Is Religion of West*, January, 1965.
  3. *Archaeological Finds Refute West's Dark Continent Views*, February, 1965.
  4. *Black Creativity Has Enriched Various Civilizations*, March, 1965.
  5. *Queen of Sheba's True Identity Confounds Historical Research*, April, 1965.

* ———, *African History Notebook*, Vol. I—*Pillars in Ethiopian History*, Howard University Press, Washington, D.C., 1981.

Vol. II—*Africa and Africans as Seen by Classical Writers*, Howard University Press, Washington, D.C., 1981.

* Harding, Vincent, *There is a River: The Black Struggles for Freedom in America*, Harcourt, Brace, Jovanovich, New York, 1981.

* Harris, Joseph E., *Africans and Their History*, Mentor Books, New American Library, paperback, New York, 1969.

* ———, *The African Presence in Asia*, Northwestern University Press, Evanston, IL, 1971.

* Hayford, E. Casely, *Gold Coast Native Institutions*, Sweet and Maxwell, London, 1903.

Henri, Florette, *Black Migration: Movement North, 1900–1920*, Anchor Press, Doubleday, New York, 1975.

* Henries, A. Doris Banks, *Africa: Our History*, Collier- Macmillan International, Toronto, 1969.

Herodotus, *The History of Herodotus*, trans. by George Rawlinson, Tudor Publishing Co., New York, 1939.

Herskovitz, Melville J., *The Myth of the Negro Past*, Beacon Press, Boston, 1958.

* Hill, Robert A., editor, *The Marcus Garvey and the Universal Negro Improvement Association Papers*, University of California Press, Berkeley, 1983. (A proposed 10 volume work).

* Hodges, Norman, E. W., *Breaking the Chains of Bondage*, Simon & Schuster, paperback, New York, 1972.

Hoffman, Eleanor, *Realm of the Evening Star, Morocco and the Land of the Moors*, Chilton Books, New York, 1965.

* Hollins, Louis, *The Life and Times of Booker T. Washington*, University of Illinois Press, Chicago.

Hooker, James R., *Black Revolutionary*, Praeger Publishers, New York, 1970.

Houston, Drusilla Dunjee, *Wonderful Ethiopians of the Ancient Cushite Empire*, Black Classic Press, Baltimore, 1985.

* Huggins, Nathan I., Kilson, Martin and Fox, Daniel M., editors, *Key Issues in the Afro-American Experience*, Vol. I & II, Harcourt, Brace and Jovanovich, New York, 1971.

* ———, *Voices from the Harlem Renaissance*, Oxford University Press, New York, 1976.

Jackson, Henry C., *The Fighting Sudanese*, MacMillan Publishing Co., London, 1954.

* Jackson, John G., *Ethiopia and the Origin of Civilization*, Black Classic Press, Baltimore, 1939.

* ———, *Introduction to African Civilizations*, Citadel Press, Secaucas, N.J., 1970.

* ———, *Man, God and Civilization*, University Books, New Hyde Park, 1970.

* ———, *Christianity Before Christ*, The Blyden Society, New York, 1938.

* James, C. L. R., *The Black Jacobins*, Vintage Books, New York, 1963.

Jenkinson, Thomas B., *Amazulu: The Zulus, their Past History, Manners, Customs, and Language, With Observations on the Country and Its Productions, Climate, etc., The Zulu War, and Zululand Since the War*, Negro Universities Press, New York, 1969.

Jordan, Winthrop D., *White Over Black*, Pelican Press, New York, 1968.

Josephy, Alvin M., Jr., editor, *The Horizon History of Africa*, American Heritage Publishing Co., New York, 1970.

July, Robert W., *A History of the African People*, Scribner's Sons Publishers, paperback, New York, 1970.

* Karenga, Maulana, *Introduction to Black Studies*, Kawaida Publications, Inglewood, CA.

Katz, William Loren, *Minorities in American History*, see Vol. I, *Early America, 1492–1812*, Franklin Watts, New York, 1974.

* King, Martin Luther, Jr., *Stride Toward Freedom, the Montgomery Story*, Ballantine Books, New York, 1958.

Kritzeck, James and Lewis, William H., editors, *Islam in Africa*, Van Nostrand-Reinhold Co., New York, 1969.

Kuhn, Alvin Boyd, *Shadow of the Third Century, A Revaluation of Christianity*, Academy Press, Elizabeth, N.J., 1949.

——, *Who is This King of Glory?*, Academy Press, Elizabeth, N.J., 1944.

Kunene, Mazisi, *Emperor Shaka the Great Zulu Epic*, Heineman and Co., London, 1979.

* Kveretwie, K. O. Bonso, *Asanti Heroes*, Oxford University Press, New York, 1964.

Lane-Poole, Stanley, *Story of the Moors in Spain*, Black Classic Press, Baltimore.

Latham, Frank B., *The Rise and Fall of "Jim Crow" 1865–1964*, F. Watts, New York, 1969.

* Lawrence, Harold G., *African Explorers of the New World*, pamphlet, NAACP Publications, New York.

Leakey, L. S. B., *The Progress and Evolution of Man in Africa*, Oxford University Press, New York, 1969.

Lemarchand, Rene, *Political Awakening in the Belgian Congo*, University of California Press, Berkeley, 1964.

Levtzion, Nehemia, *Ancient Ghana and Mali*, Methuen & Co., Ltd., London, 1973.

Lewis, Erwin and Bain, Mildred, editors, *From Freedom to Freedom: Black Roots in American Soil*, Random House, paperback, New York.

* Locke, Alain, *The New Negro,* Arno Press, New York, 1968.
* Logan, Rayford Whittingham, *The Betrayal of the Negro: From Rutherford B. Hayes to Woodrow Wilson,* Collier Books, New York, 1965.
Lugard, Flora Shaw, *A Tropical Dependency,* J. Nisbet & Co., London, 1905.
McNeil, William H., *A World History,* Oxford University Press, New York, 1967.
Maquet, Jacques, *Civilizations of Black Africa,* Oxford University Press, New York, 1972.
Massey, Gerald, *Ancient Egypt, the Light of the World,* Vols. I & II, Samuel Weiser, Inc., New York, 1970.
———, *The Natural Genesis,* Vols. I & II, Samuel Weiser, Inc., New York, 1974.
———, *A Book of the Beginnings,* Vols. I & II, Williams and Norgate Publishers, London, 1881.
* Mate, C. M. O., *A Visual History of Ghana,* Evans Bros., Ltd., paperback, London, 1964.
* Mazuri, Ali A., *The Africans, A Triple Heritage,* Little, Brown and Co., Boston, 1986.
* ———, *Protest and Power in Black Africa,* Oxford University Press, New York, 1970.
Meier, August and Rudwick, Elliott, *From Plantation to Ghetto,* Hill and Wang, New York, 1970.
* Meredith, Martin, *The First Dance of Freedom, Black America in the Post-War Era,* Harper & Row Publishers, New York, 1984.
Montagu, Ashley, editor, *The Concept of Race,* Free Press of Glencoe, New York, 1964.
Miller, Kelly, *Out of the House of Bondage,* Neale Publishing Co., New York, 1914.
Miller, William Robert, *Martin Luther King, Jr., His Life, Martyrdom and Meaning For the World,* Weybright and Talley, New York, 1968.
* Moore, Richard B., *The Name Negro—Its Origin and Evil Use,* Afro-American Publishers, New York, 1960.

Morel, E. D., *The Black Man's Burden*, Funk and Wagnalls, New York, 1905.

―――, *King Leopold's Role in Africa*, Funk and Wagnalls, New York, 1905.

―――, *Red Rubber*, Negro Universities Press, New York, 1969.

Morris, Donald R., *The Washing of the Spears*, Doubleday, New York.

* Motley, Mary Penick, *Africa: Its Empires, Nations and People*, Wayne State University Press, paperback, Detroit, 1969.

Murphy, E. Jefferson, *History of African Civilization, The People, Nations, Kingdoms and Empires of Africa from Pre-History to the Present*, Thomas Y. Crowell Co., New York.

* Nkrumah, Kwame, *Africa Must Unite*.

* ―――, *Ghana: The Autobiography of Kwame Nkrumah*.

* ―――, *Dark Days in Ghana*, Parraf Publications, Ltd., London, 1968.

Nordholt, J. W. Schulte, *The People That Walk in Darkness: A History of Black People in America*, Ballantine Books, New York, 1970.

* Ogat, B. A. and Kiernan, J. A., editors, *Zambia: A Survey of East African History*, Longmans, London, Distributed in the U.S.A. by Humanities Press, New York, 1968.

Oliver, Roland and *Atmore, Anthony, *Africa Since 1800*, Cambridge University Press, paperback, New York, 1967.

―――, editor, *The Dawn of African History*, Oxford University Press, paperback, New York.

―――, editor, *The Cambridge History of East Africa*, Cambridge University Press, New York.

Omer-Cooper, J. D., *The Zulu Aftermath*, Longmans Green & Co., London, 1966.

* Osei, G. K., *The African: His Antecedents, His Genius and His Destiny*, University Books, Syracuse, New York.

Osofsky, Gilbert, *The Burden of Race*, Harper Torch Books, New York, 1968.

* Padmore, George, *Pan-Africanism or Communism*, Doubleday Anchor Books, New York.

Patterson, Orlando, *Slavery and Social Death*, Oxford University Press, New York.

———, *Sociology of Slavery*, Oxford University Press, New York.

Pasha, Rudolf C. Slatin, *Fire and Sword in the Sudan*, Edward Arnold, New York, 1896.

Pollack, George F., *Civilizations of Africa: Historic Kingdoms, Empires and Cultures*, AEP Unit Books, American Education Publications, paperback, Middletown, CT., 1970.

* Quarles, Benjamin, *The Negro and the Making of America*, Collier Books, paperback, New York, 1969.

* ———, editor, *Frederick Douglass: Great Lives Observed*, Prentice-Hall, Inc., Englewood Cliffs, N.J.

* ———, *Black Abolitionists*, Oxford University Press, New York.

* ———, *The Negro in the American Revolution*, published for the Institute of Early American History & Culture, Williamsburg, VA, by the University of North Carolina Press, 1961.

* ———, and Stuckey, Sterling, editors, *A People Uprooted, 1500–1800*, Vol. I, Encyclopedia Britannica, Afro-American History Series, paperback, Chicago, 1969. *Chains of Slavery, 1800–1965*, Vol. II, Encyclopedia Britannica Afro-American History Series, paperback, Chicago, 1969.

Separate and Unequal, 1865–1910, Vol. III, Encyclopedia Britannica, Afro-American History Series, paperback, Chicago, 1969.

Quest for Equality, 1910 to Present, Vol. IV, Encyclopedia Britannica, Afro-American History Series, paperback, Chicago, 1971.

Ranger, T. O., editor, *Aspects of Central African History, Third World Histories*, Heinemann Educational Books, Ltd., London, 1968.

Redkey, Edwin S., *Black Exodus: Black Nationalist and Back to Africa Movements, 1890–1910*, Yale University Press, Boston, MA, 1969.

Reindorf, Carl S., *A History of the Gold Coast and Asante*, privately published, Ghana.

* Rich, Evelyn Jones and Wallerstein, Immanuel, editors, *Africa; Tradition and Change*, with Teacher's Manual, Random House, New York, 1972.

Roberts, Brian, *The Zulu Kings*, Charles Scribner's Sons, New York, 1974.

* Robins, Charlene Hill, *They Showed the Way*, Thomas Crowell, 1964.

* Rodney, Walter, *How Europe Underdeveloped Africa*, Howard University Press, Washington, D.C., 1974.

* Rogers, J. A., *World's Great Men of Color*, Vols. I & II, edited by John Henrik Clarke, Collier-MacMillan, paperback, New York, 1972.

* ———, *Sex and Race*, Privately published by Rogers Publishing Co., c/o Mrs. J. A. Rogers, St. Petersburg, VA.

Rosenthal, Ricky, *The Splendor That was Africa*, Oceana Publications, Inc., Dobbs Ferry, New York, 1967.

Rotberg, Robert I. and * Mazuri, Ali, editors, *Protest and Power in Black Africa*, Oxford University Press, New York.

Roucek, Joseph S., *The Negro Impact on Western Civilization*, Philosophical Library, New York, 1970.

Roux, Robert, *Time Longer Than Rope*, University of Wisconsin Press, paperback.

* Samkange, Stanlake, *African Saga: A Brief Introduction to African History*, Abingdon Press, Nashville, TN.

Sanford, Eva., *The Mediterranean World in Ancient Times*, Ronald Press Co., New York, 1938.

* Sarbah, John Mansah, *Fanti Customary Lore*, F. Cass, Ltd., London.

Schwartz, Barry N. and Disch, Robert, *White Racism*, Dell Publishing Co., New York, 1970.

Segal, Ronald, *The Race War*, Viking Press, New York, 1967.

Shinnie, Margaret, *Ancient African Kingdoms*, St. Martin's Press, New York, 1965.

Silverberg, Robert, *Empires in the Dust, Ancient Civilizations Brought to Light*, Chilton Books, Philadelphia, PA, 1963.

———, *Akhnaten, The Rebel Pharaoh*, Chilton Books, Philadelphia, PA, 1964.

* Simmons, William J., *Men of Mark, Eminent, Progressive and Rising*, Johnson Publishing Co., Chicago, 1970.

Slade, Ruth, *King Leopold's Congo*, Oxford University Press, New York, 1962.

Smith, Adam, *Nubia: Corridor to Africa*, Princeton University Press, Princeton, N.J.

Smith, G. Elliot, *The Ancient Egyptians and the Origin of Civilization*, Harper and Brothers, London, 1923.

Snyder, Louis L., *The Idea of Racialism*, Van-Nostrand, New York, 1962.

* Snowden, Frank M., Jr., *Blacks in Antiquity . . . Ethiopians in the Greco-Roman Experience*, The Belnap Press, Harvard University, Cambridge, Mass., 1970.

Sordo, Enrique, *Moorish Spain, Cordoba, Seville, Granada*, Crown Publishers, New York, 1963.

* Sterling, Dorothy, *Tear Down the Walls*, New American Library, New York, 1970.

Tannenbaum, Frank, *Slave and Citizen, the Negro in the Americas*, Vintage Books, New York, 1946.

Tappin, Edgar A., *Blacks in America: Then and Now*, Christian Science Monitor, paperback, Boston, 1969.

Tarikh, Vol. 1, No. 3, Humanities Press, New York, 1966.

Terkel, Studs, *Hard Times, An Oral History of the Great Depression*, Pantheon Books, New York, 1970.

Thompson, Vincent Bakpetu, *Africa and Unity: The Evolution of Pan-Africanism*, Longmans Green and Co.l, Ltd., London, 1969.

* Thorpe, Dr. Earl E., editor, *The Black Experience in America*, a series of 10 pamphlets on Afro-American History, American Education Publishers, Columbus, Ohio, 1972.

* Van Sertima, Dr. Ivan, *They Came Before Columbus*, Random House, New York, 1976.

* ———, editor, The Journal of African Civilization, Rutgers University, New Jersey. See special issues:
Africans in Early Asia.

Africans in Early Europe.

Vansina, Jan, *Kingdoms of the Savanna*, University of Wisconsin Press, Madison, 1966.

Vincent, Theodore G., *Black Power and the Garvey Movement*, The Ramparts Press, Berkeley, CA.

Von Wuthenau, *The Art of Terracotta Pottery in Pre-Columbian Central and South America*, Crown Publishers, New York, 1965.

Wiltse, David, Intro., *David Walker's Appeal*, Hill and Wang, New York, 1965.

* Washington, Booker T., *Up From Slavery*, Dell Publishing Co., New York.

Weatherwax, John M., *Picture History of Africa*, pamphlet.

————, *The Man Who Stole a Continent*, pamphlet.

* Webster, J. B., Boahen, A. A. and Idowuy, H. O., *The Growth of African Civilization: The Revolutionary Year: West Africa Since 1800*, Longmans Green and Co., Ltd., London.

Welch, Galbraith, *North African Prelude, the First Seven Thousand Years*, William Morrow and Co., Ltd., London.

Weiner, Leo, *Africa in the Discovery of America*, Innes & Sons, Philadelphia, 1922.

* Williams, Chancellor, *The Destruction of Black Civilization: Great Issues of a Race from 4500 B.C. to 2000 A.D.*, Third World Press, Chicago, 1974.

* Williams, Bruce, *The Lost Pharaohs of Nubia*, Archaeology Magazine.

* Williams, Eric, *Capitalism and Slavery*, Capricorn Books, paperback, New York, 1966.

————, *From Columbus to Castro: The History of the Caribbean, 1492–1969*, Harper & Row, New York, 1970.

————, *Documents in West Indian History*, PNM Publishing Co., Port of Spain, Trinidad, 1963.

* Williams, George Washington, *A History of the Negro Race in the United States*, Vol. 1, Bergman Publishers, New York, 1968.

Willis, A. J., *An Introduction to the History of Central Africa*, Oxford University Press, New York, 1967.

Wilson, John A., *The Culture of Ancient Egypt*, Phoenix Books, University of Chicago Press, 1951.

Wingfield, R. J., *The Story of Old Ghana, Melle and Songhai*, Cambridge University Press, New York, 1957.

Wolters, Raymond, *Negroes and the Great Depression, the Problem of Economic Recovery*, Greenwood Publishing Co., Westport, CT, 1970.

* Woodson, Carter G. and Wesley, Charles H., *The Negro in our History*, Associated Publishers, Inc., Washington, D.C., 1962.

* ———, *The Story of the Negro Retold*, Associated Publishers, Inc., Washington, D.C., 1959.

* ———, *Negro Makers of History*, Associated Publishers, Inc., Washington, D.C., 1958.

* ———, *African Background Outlined*, Afro-American Studies Series, New American Library, paperback, New York, 1969.

* ———, *African Heroes and Heroines*, Associated Publishers, Inc., paperback, Washington, D.C., 1969.

Woodward, C. Vann, *The Burden of Southern History*, Louisiana State University Press, Baton Rouge, 1968.

———, *The Strange Career of "Jim Crow"*, Oxford University Press, New York, 1966.

In the study of African History there is a need to also have some knowledge of World History, especially the history of Europe. The following books are recommended for orientation on this broader aspect of history.

Wells, H. G., *The Outline of History*, Doubleday Publishing Co., New York, 1949.

Palmer, R. R. and Colton, Joel, *A History of the Modern World*, third edition, Alfred A. Knopf, New York, 1968.

McNeill, William H., *A World History*, Oxford University Press, New York, 1967.

General References

1. THE NEW NEGRO, edited by Alain Locke, reprinted by Atheneum Press, New York, 1968
2. A GUIDE TO STUDIES IN AFRICAN HISTORY, by Willis N. Huggins and John G. Jackson, Wyllie Press, New York, 1934
3. AN INTRODUCTION TO AFRICAN CIVILIZATIONS WITH MAIN CURRENTS IN ETHIOPIAN HISTORY, by Willis N. Huggins and John G. Jackson, Negro University Press, New York, 1969 (reprint)
4. WAS JESUS CHRIST A NEGRO? and THE AFRICAN ORIGINS OF THE MYTHS AND LEGENDS OF THE GARDEN OF EDEN, by John G. Jackson, ECA Associates, 1987 (reprint)
5. PAGAN ORIGINS OF THE CHRIST MYTH, by John G. Jackson, The Truthseeker Company, 1976 (reprint)
6. THE NEGRO IN OUR HISTORY, by Carter G. Woodson, The Associated Publishers Inc., Washington, D.C., 1922 (revised and reprinted, 1962)
7. THE AFRICAN BACKGROUND OUTLINED, by Carter G. Woodson, The Associated Publishers Inc., Washington, D.C., 1936
8. WORLD'S GREAT MEN OF COLOR, Vol. I & II, MacMillan and Co., New York, 1972 (reprint)
9. THE HUMAN SIDE OF A PEOPLE AND THE RIGHT NAME, by Raphael Philemon Powell, The Philemon Company, New York, 1937
10. AFRICAN ORIGINS OF CIVILIZATION: MYTH OR REALITY, by Cheikh Anta Diop, Lawrence Hill and Co., Westport, Connecticut, 1974
11. PRE-COLONIAL BLACK AFRICA, by Cheikh Anta

Diop, Lawrence Hill and Co., Westport, Connecticut, 1987

12. BLACK AFRICA: THE ECONOMIC AND CULTURAL BASIS FOR A FEDERATED STATE, by Cheikh Anta Diop, Lawrence Hill and Co., Westport, Connecticut, 1978

13. THE CULTURAL UNITY OF BLACK AFRICA, by Cheikh Anta Diop, Third World Press, Chicago, 1978.

There is an educational crisis in African-American communities today. For at least a generation some parents have left the responsibility for the education of our young to a school system that at best is poorly prepared and at worst has little expertise in educating children of African ancestry toward freedom . . . Education that engenders oppresssion and dependency is not appropiate to teach liberation . . . Reclaiming the education of our young is within our capacity.

(Adelaide Sanford)

Curriculum Aids and Background Readings
BY LARRY OBADELE WILLIAMS

Adams, William E. (1970) "Black Studies in the Elementary Schools," *Journal of Negro Education*, 39, Summer, pp. 202–8

Akbar, Na'im (1988) *Chains and Images of Psychological Slavery*, N.J.: New Mind Productions

Akbar, Na'im (1981) "Cultural Expressions of the African-American Child," *Black Child Journal*, Vol. 2, No. 2, pp. 6–15

Alexander, Rae (1970) "What is a Racist Book?" *Inter-Racial Books for Children*, 3, Autumn, 1,5,7

Are You Going to Teach About Africa? Prepared by the School Services Division of the African-American Institute, New York: African-American Institute, 1969

Baker, August (1969) "Guidelines for Black Books: An Open Letter to Juvenile Editors," *Publishers Weekly*, 196, July 14, pp. 131–133

Baldwin, Joseph A. (1987) "African Psychology and Black Personality Testing," *The Negro Educational Review*, Vol. XXXVIII, April-July, Nos. 2–3, pp. 56–66

Baldwin, Joseph A. (1985) "Psychological Aspects of European Cosmology In American Society," *The Western Journal of Black Studies*, Vol. 9, No. 4, pp. 216–223

Banks, James A. (1988) "Education, Citizenship, and Cultural Options," *Education and Society*, Spring, pp. 19–22

Banks, James A. (ED) (1981) *Multiethnic Education: Theory in Practice*, Boston, MA: Allyn & Bacon.

Banks, James A. (1970) "Developing Racial Tolerance with Literature on the Black Inner-City," *Social Education*, 34, May, pp. 549–52

Banks, James A. (1969) "Relevant Social Studies for Black Pupils," *Social Education*, 33, January, pp. 66–69

Barringer, Felicity (1990) "Scholarly Arguments for a Black Heritage: Africa's Claim to Egypt's History Grows More Insistent," *New York Times*, Sunday, February 4, p. 6E

Ben-Jochannan, Yosef (1990) *Cultural Genocide and the Black African Studies Curriculum*, Newport, VA: ECA Associates

Bernal, Martin (1987) *Black Athena: The Afro Asiatic Roots of Classical Civilization*, Vol. I: The Fabrication of Ancient Greece 1785–1985, N.J.: Rutgers University Press

Birtha, J. M. (1969) "Portrayal of the Black in Children's Literature," *Pennsylvania Library Association Bulletin*, 24, July, pp. 189–97

Boggs, Grace Lee (1974) "Education: The Great Obsession," In *Education and Black Struggle: Notes from the Colonized World* (Ed.) Institute of the Black World, Mass.: Harvard Educational Review, pp. 61–81

Brown, Gayleatha B. (1970) *Trends in the Presentation of Africa in Selected Children's Literature in English 1930–1969*, Washington, D.C., Howard University, Unpublished Master's Thesis

Brown, Lalage (1970) "Children's Books from Africa," *Interracial Books for Children*, 2, Spring, pp. 1, 4–6, 8

Brown, Sterling A. (1982) "Negro Characters As Seen by White Authors," *Callaloo*, Vol. 5, Nos. 1 & 2, Feb.–May, pp. 55–105

Bulhan, Hussein Abdilahi (1985) *Frantz Fanon and the Psychology of Oppression*, New York: Plenum Press

Butler, Joan E. (1972) "Audiovisual Aids for the Study of Africa: A Selected Guide to New Materials for Children and Young Adults: 1970–1971," A *Current Bibliography On African Affairs*, Vol. 5, Series II, pp. 185–99.

Cabral, Amilcar (1973) *Return to the Source: Selected Speeches of Amilcar Cabral*, New York: Monthly Review Press

Carew, Jan R. (1984) "The Indian African Presence in the Americas: Some Aspects of Historical Distortion," In *Ex-*

pressions of Power in Education: Studies of Class, Gender and Race (Ed.) Edgar B. Gumbert, Atlanta, Georgia State University, pp. 51–67

Carew, Jan R. (1988) "Columbus and the Origins of Racism in the Americas: Part One," *Race and Class*, XXIX, No. 4, pp. 1–19

Carnoy, Martin (1974) *Education as Cultural Imperialism*, New York: David McKay Company, Inc.

Chinweizu (1977) "Education for Power: Making Ethnicity Work," *First World*, Vol. 1, No. 3, May/June, pp. 20–24

Chinweizu (1988) *Voices from Twentieth Century Africa: Griots and Towncriers*, Boston: Faber and Faber

Clegg, Legrand H. (1981) "The First Invaders," *Journal of African Civilizations*, Vol. 3, No. 1, April, pp. 8–20

Clegg, Legrand H. (1980) "Black Royalty in the Pacific," *Uraeus: The Journal of Unconscious Life*, Winter Solstice Issue, Vol. 2, No. 1, pp. 35–38

Clegg, Legrand H. and Lisbeth Gant (1978) "The Black Roots of King Tut," *Black Collegian*, Vol. 8, No. 3, Jan/Feb, pp. 41, 44, 81

Clegg, Legrand H. (1972) "Ancient America: A Missing Link in Black History?" *A Current Bibliography on African Affairs*, Vol. 5, No. 3, Series I, May, pp. 286–319

Cox, Clinton (1990) "Whites Only: The Weapon of Education History," *New York City Sun Newspaper*, Feb. 21–27, pp. 6–7, 34

Cox, Clinton (1990) "Diane Ravitch: Who is This Woman and Why is She Smiling?" *New York City Sun Newspaper*, March 14–20, pp. 9, 34–35

Crawford, Marc (1961) "The Scholar Nobody Knows (William Leo Hansberry)," *Ebony*, May, pp. 59–68

Crossey, J. M. D. (1970) "Building a Working Collection on Africa: Note on Bibliographic Aids and Dealers," *Africana Library Journal*, 1, Summer, pp. 18–22

Diggs, Irene (1976) "W. E. B. DuBois and Children," *Phylon*, 37, December, pp. 370–399

Erny, Pierre (1968) *Childhood and Cosmos: The Social Psy-*

chology of the Black African Child, New York: New
Perspectives

Fenton, Edwin (1969) "Crispus Attucks is Not Enough: The
Social Studies and Black Americans" *Social Education,*
33, April, pp. 396–99

Furniss, W. T. (1969) "Racial Minorities and Curriculum
Change," *Educational Record L* (Fall), pp. 360–70

Galo, Maria T. (1988) "Dr. Sizemore Challenges Multicultural
Counselors," *Black Issues in Higher Education,* April 15,
pp. 5, 20

Hale, Janice E. (1977) "De-Mythicizing The Education of
Black Children," *First World,* Vol. 1, No. 3, May/June,
pp. 30–35

Hare, Nathan (1969) "The Teaching of Black History and
Culture in the Secondary Schools," *Social Education,* 33,
April, pp. 385–88

Harris, Nelson H. (1969), "The Treatment of Negroes in
Books and Media Designed for the Elementary School,"
Social Education, 33, April, pp. 434–37

Henry, William A. (1990) "Beyond the Melting Pot," *Time
Magazine,* April 9, pp. 28–31

Hilliard, Asa G. (1989) "The Socialization of Our Children for
the Resurrection of African People," Unpublished paper.

Hilliard, Asa G. (1990) "Promoting African-American Student
Achievement," School/College Collaboration: Teaching
At-Risk Youth, Conference Proceedings, Washington,
D.C.: Council of Chief State School Officers

Hilliard, Asa G. (1986) "Pedagogy in Ancient KMT," in Mau-
lana Karenga and Jacob Carruthers (Eds.) *Kemet and the
Africa Worldview,* Los Angeles: University of Sankore
Press, pp. 131–148

Hilliard, Asa G. (1986) *Free Your Mind: Return to the Source
African Origins: A Selected Bibliography (Classified) and
Outline on African-American History from Ancient Times
to the Present: A Resource Packet,* Atlanta: Waset
Productions.

Hilliard, Asa G. (1986) *Race and Education: A Search for Legitimacy Revisited,* Texas: Texas Southern University.

Hilliard, Asa G. (1985) "Kemetic Concepts in Education," In Ivan Van Sertima (Ed.) *Nile Valley Civilizations: Journal of African Civilizations,* pp. 153-162.

Hilliard, Asa G. (1985) "The Meaning of KMT (Ancient Egyptian) History for the Contemporary African-American Experience," Unpublished Manuscript. pp. 1-17.

Hilliard, Asa G. (1982) "The Maroons Within Us: The Lessons of Africa for the Parenting and Education of African-American Children," Memphis: Memphis State University.

Hilliard, Asa G. (1977) "Intellectual Strengths of Minority Children" In D. Cross, G. Baker, L. States (Eds.) *Teachings in a Multicultural Society,* New York: Free Press.

Horn, Miriam (1989) "The Reawakening of American Music," *U.S. News & World Report,* Nov. 27, pp. 68-70.

Jablonsky, Adelaide (1970) "Media for Teaching Afro-American Studies," *ICRD Bulletin,* 6, Spring/Summer, pp. 1-23.

Johnson, Edwina (1969) "Black History: The Early Childhood," *School Library Journal,* 15, May, pp. 43-44.

Jones, Rhett S. (1971) "Proving Blacks Inferior, 1870-1930," *Black World,* February, pp. 419-.

Krauthammer, Charles (1990) "Education: Doing Bad and Feeling Good," *Time,* February 5, p. 78.

Kent, George E. (1973) "George Kent Interviews Chancellor Williams," *The Black Position,* No. 3, pp. 17-19.

Leo, John (1989) "Teaching History the Way it Happened," *U.S. News and World Report,* November 27, p. 73.

Lumpkin, Beatrice (1990) "Ancient Egypt for Children-Facts, Fiction and Lies," In Ivan Van Sertima (Ed.) *Egypt Revisited,* New Brunswick: Transaction Publishers, pp. 416-424.

Lumpkin, Beatrice (1985) "Mathematics and Engineering in the Nile Valley," In Ivan Van Sertima (Ed.) *Nile Valley Civilizations,* N.J.: Transaction Books, pp. 102-119.

Malcomson, Scott L. (1989) "How the West Was Lost: Writing at the End of the World," Voice Literary Supplement, April, pp. 11–14.

Maren, Michael (1989) "A Walk on the White Side: Postcolonials Reclaim the Dark Continent," Voice Literary Supplement, April, pp. 15–16.

Martin, Michael (1975) "The Functions of Colonial Education: On Dialectics, Ideology and Dehumanization," Black World, August, pp. 4–16.

McIntyre, Charshee Charlotte-Lawrence and Davidson, Douglas V. (1988, May 6) Minority Multicultural Education: Suggestions for Content and Appropriate Pedagogy. A paper presented at the George Mason University's 5th Annual Conference on Non- Traditional and Interdisciplinary Programs, Virginia Beach, Virginia.

Mills, Joyce White (1978–79) The Black World in Literature for Children: A Bibliography of Print and Non-Print Materials, Vol. IV, Atlanta: School of Library and Information Studies, Atlanta University.

Morris, Darrell (1990) "School Curriculum Revisions Face Implementation Hurdles: Departure from Eurocentric Emphasis Often Resisted," Black Issues in Higher Education, March 15, p. 11.

Meier, August and Rudwick, Elliott (1986) Black History and the Historical Profession 1915–1980, Chicago: University of Illinois Press.

Nichols, Edwin J. (1986) "Cultural Foundations for Teaching Black Children," In Oswald M. T. Ratteray (Ed.) Teaching Mathematics, Vol. I: Culture, Motivation, History and Classroom Management, Washington, D.C.: Institute for Independent Education, pp. 1–7.

Nix, Kemie (1988) "Fiction Can Teach Black History Without Boring Kids," The Atlanta Journal/Constitution Newspaper, February 28, p. 8.

Nobles, Wade (1987) "Psychometrics and African-American Reality: A Question of Cultural Antimony," The Negro

Educational Review, Vol. XXXVIII, April–July, Nos. 2–3, pp. 45–55.

Nobles, Wade (1973) "Psychological Research and the Black Self-Concept: A Critical Review," *Journal of Social Issues*, 29, 1, pp. 11–31.

"Not Just in February: Teaching African and African-American Contributions Throughout the Year Across the Curriculum," *SEF NEWS* (Southern Education Foundation), Vol. 4, No. 2, October, 1989, pp. 1–2.

Petrie, Phil (1981) "Dr. Chancellor Williams: Celebrating Our Glorious History," *Essence*, December, pp. 74–139

Piliawsky, Mont (1982) *Exit 13: Oppression and Racism in Academia*, Boston: South End Press.

Preiswerk, Roy and D. Perrot (1978) *Ethnocentrism and History: Africa, Asia and Indian America in Western Textbooks*, New York: NOK Publishers International.

Robinson, Carrie (1969) "Media for the Black Curriculum," *American Library Association Bulletin*, 63, February, pp. 242–46.

Roth, Rodney W. (1970) "Critique of Development in Black Studies at the Elementary Level," *Journal of Negro Education*, 33, Summer, pp. 230–38.

Saakana, Amon S. and A. Pearse (1986) *Towards the decolonization of the British Educational System*, London: Karnak House.

Sandoval, Valerie (1978) "The Brand of History: A Historiographic Account of the Work of J. A. Rogers," *Center for Research in Black Culture Journal*, Spring, Vol. 1, No. 4, pp. 5–19.

Saving the African-American Child: A Report of the National Alliance of Black School Educators, Inc. Task Force on Black Academic and Cultural Excellence, Washington, D.C.: National Alliance of Black School Educators, Inc. (November 1984).

"Say Yes Through Family Math," *Cultural Connections*: 1988, Washington, D.C.: National Urban Coalition.

Sinette, Elinor D. (1965) "The Brownies' Book: A Pioneer Publication for Children," *Freedomways*, Vol, no. 1.

Sizemore, Barbara A. (1990) "The Politics of Curriculum, Race and Class," *Journal of Negro Education*, Vol. 59, No. 1, pp. 77–85.

Sizemore, Barbara A. (1973A) "Separatism: A Reality Approach to Inclusion?" in Edgar G. Epps (Ed.) *Race Relations*, (pp. 305–331), Cambridge, MA: Winthrop Publishers.

Sizemore, Barbara A. (1973B) "Making the School a Vehicle for Cultural Pluralism," in Madelon D. Stent, William B. Hazard and Harry N. Rivlin (Eds.) *Cultural Pluralism in Education: A Mandate for Change* (pp. 43–54), New York: Appleton- Century Crofts.

Spady, James G. (1986) "The Changing Perception of C. A. Diop and His Work: The Pre-Eminence of a Scientific Spirit," in Ivan Van Sertima and Larry Williams (Eds.) *Great African Thinkers*, Vol. I: Cheikh Anta Diop, N.J.: Transaction Books, pp. 89–101.

Spady, James G. (1975) "The Cultural Unity of Cheikh Anta Diop: 1948–1964," *Black Book's Bulletin*, Vol. 3, Spring, pp. 28–35, 80–84.

Spady, James G. (1970) "Dr. William Leo Hansberry: The Legacy of an African Hunter," *A Current Bibliography on African Affairs*, Nov/Dec., pp. 25–40.

Steele, Ronald D. (1990) "Africentricity: Attaining our Own Identity," *Players*, Vol. 16, Number 10, March, pp. 4–7, 46.

Steele, Ronald D. (N.D.) "African-American: Know Thyself," *Players*, pp. 46–48, 50–51.

Tate, Greg (1989) "History: The Colorized Version or Everything You Learned in School Was Wrong," *Village Voice*, March 28, pp. 48–50.

Thiong'O, Ngugi Wa (1986) *Decolonising the Mind: The Politics of Language in African Literature*, New Hampshire: Heinemann Educational Books.

Thiong'O, Ngugi Wa (1983) *Barrell of a Pen: Resistance to*

Repression in Neo-Colonial Kenya, New Jersey: Africa World Press.

Thompson, Judith and Gloria Woodward (1969) "Black Perspective in Books for Children," *Wilson Library Bulletin*, 44, Dec., pp. 416–24.

Turner, W. Burghardt (1975) "J. A. Rogers: Portrait of an Afro-American Historian," *The Black Scholar*, Jan/Feb., Vol. 6, No. 5, pp. 32–39.

Walker, Sheila S. (1980–81) *Images of Africa in the Oakland Public Schools: Assessment of Educational Media Resources Pertaining to Africa*, California: University of California School of Education.

White, Betsy (1989) "Portland, Ore. Schools Lead Way in Teaching Black Culture in Every Classroom," *The Atlanta Journal and Constitution*, Sunday, January 29, p. 4.

White, Betsy (1989) "City Schools Skim Over Black History," *The Atlanta Journal and Constitution*, Sunday, January 29, p. 1A, 14A.

Williams, Larry Obadele (1990) *Critical References for Infusing African and African-American Studies in the Atlanta Public Schools*, Atlanta: Atlanta Public Schools.

Williams, Larry Obadele (1989) "Infusing African and African-American Content in the School Curriculum: A New Cultural Offensive," *Talking Drums*, Nov./Dec., p. 11, 22.

Williams, Larry Obadele (1989) "Black History in White America: Retracing Our Roots and Demanding Our Legacy," *Fast Forward Magazine*, pp. 44–45.

Woodson, Carter G. (1933) *The Miseducation of the Negro*, Washington, D.C.: Associated Publishers.

Wright, Bobby E. (1976) "A Psychological Theory of Educating the Black Child," *Black Books Bulletin*, vol. 4, No. 3, Fall, pp. 12–16.

Additional References

Bernal, M. (1987). *Black Athena: The Afroasiatic Roots of Classical Civilization: Volume I. The Fabrication of Ancient Greece.* London: Free Association Books.

Benedict, R. (1945). *Race: Science and Politics.* New York: Viking.

Chase, A. (1977). *The Legacy of Malthus: The Social Cost of Scientific Racism.* New York: Alfred A. Knopf.

Blauner, R. (1972). *Racial Oppression in America.* New York: Harper and Row.

Bloom, A. (1987) *The Closing of the American Mind: How Higher Education Had Democracy and Impoverished the Souls of Today's Students.* New York: Simon and Schuster.

Davidson, B. (1984). *Africa* [Videotape Series]. Massachusetts: Home Vision.

Forbes, J. D. (1977). *Racism, Scholarship and Cultural Pluralism Higher Education.* David, CA: University of California Native American Studies Tecumseh Center.

Gould, S. (1981). *The Mismeasure of Man.* New York: W. W. Norton & Co.

Guthrie, R. W. (1976). *Even the Rat Was White: A Historical View of Psychology.* New York: Harper & Row.

Hirsch, E. D., Jr. (1987). *Cultural Literacy: What Eery American Needs to Know.* Boston: Houghton Mifflin.

"Historians blamed for perpetuating bias-outgoing president challenges colleague." (1987). *Black Issues in Higher Education, 4*(4), 2.

Hodge, J. L., Struckmann, D. K., & Trost, L. D. (1975). *Cultural Bases of Racism and Group Oppression: An Examination of Traditional "Western" Concepts, Values and In-*

stitutional *Structures Which Support Racism, Sexism and Elitism.* Berkeley, CA: Two Riders Press.

Jacobs, P., Landau, S., & Pell, E. (1971). *To Serve the Devil: Volume II. Colonials and Sojourners: A Documentary History of America's Racial History and Why It Has Been Kept Hidden.* New York: Vantage Books.

Kamin, L. (1974). *The Science and Politics of IQ.* New York: John Wiley & Sons.

Montague, A. (Ed.). (1987). *The Concept of the Primitive.* New York: The Free Press.

Pearce, R. H. (1965). *Savagism and Civilization: A Study of the Indian and the American Mind.* Baltimore: John Hopkins.

Stanton, W. (1960). *The Leopard's Spots: Scientific Attitudes Toward Race in America 181–59.* Chicago: University of Chicago Press.

Van Sertima, I. (1989). *Egypt Revisited.* New Brunswick: Transaction Press.

Weinreich, M. (1946). *Hitler's Professors: The Part of Scholarship in Germany's Crimes Against the Jewish People.* New York: Yiddish Scientific Institute-YIVO.

CONFERENCE COORDINATOR

Dr. Herman L. Reese
Conference Coordinator
Consultant – Southern Education Foundation

An exemplary educator, counselor and academic administrator, Dr. Reese for the past twenty years has been influential in implementing programs that address emerging issues in higher education, and the social and economic gains of Black Americans and others. He is Conference Coordinator, National Conference on the Infusion of African and African American Content in the School Curriculum; Consultant, The College Board and Director of the Black College Library Improvement Project.

EDITORS

Asa G. Hilliard III

Asa G. Hilliard III is the Fuller E. Calloway Professor of Urban Education at Georgia State University, Atlanta, Georgia. He holds a joint appointment in the Department of Educational Foundations and the Department of Counseling and Psychological Services. Dr. Hilliard served previously as a department chairman and a Dean of the School of Education at San Francisco State University. In addition to his work as an educational psychologist, he has specialized in the study of Ancient African Civilizations, especially Ancient Kemet. Dr. Hilliard has published widely on many topics including co-authoring with Dr. Barbara Sizemore, *Saving the African American Child: A Report of the National Alliance of Black School Educators.*

Lucretia Payton-Stewart

Lucretia Payton-Stewart is an Associate Professor at Georgia State University, Atlanta, Georgia. For the past twenty years, Dr. Payton-Stewart has worked in the field of private and public higher education focusing on leadership development and curriculum instruction. She has served on numerous task forces and panels relating to teacher education, technology, leadership development and multicultural education. She serves as a consultant in higher education evaluating public schools and higher institutions of learning. She has served as a classroom teacher in the Detroit Public School System whereby she coordinated the Intercultural Curriculum. As lead consultant trainer for Educational Opportunity Centers, she co-authored Leadership manuals, authored *Modules on Management Theories and Practices*. Her most recent publication is with Children's Press, where she has written two volumes of Teacher Manuals for the Multiethnic Heritage 1st African American Studies Series to be released in the fall of 1990. In October 1989 she served as Co-Director, National Conference on the Infusion of African and African American Content in the School Curriculum.

Larry Obadele Williams

Larry Obadele Williams has had wide experience in the field of African and African American studies. As a historian, researcher and lecturer, he has been published in *Afrika Must Unite: A Journal of Modern African Affairs*, the *Journal of African Civilizations*, *Talking Drum and Fast Forward Magazine*. Mr. Williams has been instrumental in organizing numerous conferences such as *The Return to the Source Conference 1983*, *The Nile Valley Conference 1984*, the *Southern Regional Kemetic Studies Conference 1986* and the *Sixth Annual ASCAC African Civilizations Conference 1989*. He has served as Co-convener of the Bennu Study Group, Board member and Southern Regional President of the Association for the Study of Classical African Civilizations (ASCAC). As an Author and Editor, he is the co-author of the article, "Great Queens of Ethiopia," published in *Black Women in Antiquity* edited by Ivan Van Sertima; co-edited *The Teachings of Ptahhotep: The Oldest Book in the World* with Asa G. Hilliard III and Nia Damali; *Great African Thinkers, Vol. I: Cheikh Anta Diop* with Ivan Van Sertima. Currently, he is an African and African American Curriculum Content Specialist for the Atlanta Public Schools.

HIGHLIGHTS

Dr. John Henrik Clarke at 1st National Conference On the Infusion of African and African American Content in the School Curriculum, October 1989.

Dr. Ivan Van Sertima, Rutgers University answers questions at Infusion Conference.

Left to Right—Joyce B. Harris, and Atlanta Public School Teachers

Left to Right—Dr. Lucretia Payton-Stewart, (Ga. State University), Dr. J. Jerome Harris, Superintendent (Atlanta Public Schools), Dr. Wade W. Nobles and Dr. Asa G. Hilliard III (Georgia State University).

Infusion Conference Group Shot October 1989

Larry Obadele Williams, African Research Specialist, conducting Infusion Workshop.

(Left to Right) Mrs. Gladys Twyman, Coordinator African American Infusion Program, Dr. Mae A. Kendall, Director, Atlanta Public Schools.

Left to Right—Dr. Herman L. Reese, Southern Education Foundation, Dr. Myrtice N. Taylor, Assistant Superintendent, Atlanta Public Schools and Dr. Lucretia Payton-Stewart, Georgia State University.

(Left to Right) Jeff Dickerson (Atlanta Constitution Newspaper), Dr. Asa G. Hilliard III, Dr. Ronald H. Lewis, Dr. John S. Blackshear, Dr. Lucretia Payton-Stewart, Dr. J. Jerome Harris and _____ _____.